Building & Finishing

Walls & Ceilings

- *Drywall* • *Paneling* • *Ceiling tile*
- *Wallcovering* • *Trim moldings* • *Texturing*

CREATIVE PUBLISHING international

CHANHASSEN, MINNESOTA

www.creativepub.com

Contents

© Copyright 2002
Creative Publishing international, Inc.
18705 Lake Drive East
Chanhassen, Minnesota 55317
1-800-328-3895
www.creativepub.com
All rights reserved

Printed by Quebecor World
10 9 8 7 6 5 4 3 2 1

President/CEO: Michael Eleftheriou
Vice President/Publisher: Linda Ball
Vice President/Retail Sales & Marketing: Kevin Haas

Executive Editor: Bryan Trandem
Creative Director: Tim Himsel
Managing Editor: Michelle Skudlarek
Editorial Director: Jerri Farris

Author & Lead Editor: Philip Schmidt
Senior Art Director: David Schelitzche
Editors: Barbara Harold, Thomas G. Lemmer
Copy Editor: Tracy Stanley
Technical Photo Editor: Paul Gorton
Illustrator: David Schelitzche
Photo Researchers: Julie Caruso, Angela Hartwell
Studio Services Manager: Jeanette Moss McCurdy
Photo Team Leader: Tate Carlson

Photographers: Tate Carlson, Andrea Rugg
Scene Shop Carpenters: Randy Austin, Shawn Jensen
Director of Production Services: Kim Gerber

BUILDING & FINISHING WALLS & CEILINGS
Created by: The Editors of Creative Publishing international, Inc.,
in cooperation with Black & Decker. Black & Decker® is a trademark
of The Black & Decker Corporation and is used under license.

Other titles from Creative Publishing international include:
*New Everyday Home Repairs, Decorating With Paint & Wallcovering, Basic
Wiring & Electrical Repairs, Advanced Home Wiring, Landscape Design &
Construction, Bathroom Remodeling, Built-In Projects for the Home,
Refinishing & Finishing Wood, Home Masonry Repairs & Projects, Building
Porches & Patios, Flooring Projects & Techniques, Advanced Home
Plumbing, Remodeling Kitchens, Carpentry: Remodeling, Carpentry:
Tools•Walls•Shelves•Doors, Great Decks, Building Decks, Advanced Deck
Building, Stonework & Masonry Projects, Finishing Basements & Attics,
Sheds, Gazebos & Outbuildings, Customizing Your Home, The Complete
Guide to Home Plumbing, The Complete Guide to Home Wiring, The Com-
plete Guide to Building Decks, The Complete Guide to Painting & Decorat-
ing, The Complete Guide to Creative Landscapes, The Complete Guide to
Home Masonry, The Complete Guide to Home Carpentry, The Complete
Guide to Home Storage, The Complete Photo Guide to Home Repair, The
Complete Photo Guide to Home Improvement, The Complete Photo Guide
to Outdoor Home Improvement.*

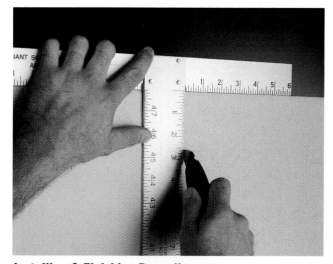

Installing & Finishing Drywall. 41

Library of Congress
Cataloging-in-Publication Data

ISBN 1-58923-042-6

Finishing Walls & Ceilings 71

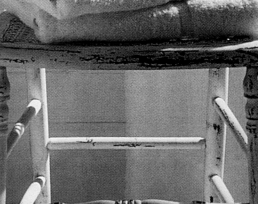

Introduction

As homeowners, we change our walls and ceilings more frequently than any other parts of our homes. Perhaps it's because the results of our efforts can be quite dramatic for relatively little work (just think of how a new coat of paint brings a sense of renewal). Or we change them because, over time, we simply grow tired of our surroundings. Whatever the motivation, these improvements become part of a never-ending endeavor to make our interior spaces more beautiful, comfortable, and personal. This book can help you in that endeavor, whether you're merely adding accent trim or building a whole new wall.

New walls can make an enormous difference in how a space is used. They can alter traffic flow, provide privacy, add storage space, and create intimate nooks within large, open areas. Building walls is well within the skill level and budget of most do-it-yourselfers, and this book shows you how to construct walls with wood, steel, and glass block.

You'll also find everything you need to know about drywall. A great material for remodeling, drywall is inexpensive and easy to install or repair, and it finishes to a smooth, flat surface that's perfect for paint or wallcovering. If smoothness is not what you're after, you can add a surface texture to drywall, as a decorative treatment or to match existing plaster walls.

When it comes to decorating your walls and ceilings, there are many finishing tools and techniques to work with. You can use paint to make a small room seem larger and more airy, or to do just the opposite with a large, impersonal room. The same possibilities apply to ceilings, where a smooth, light-colored finish expands the visual space, while a heavier treatment, like tile or paneling, makes a room more intimate. Adding a wainscot or crown molding can transform a plain or boxy interior, and a faux-finish can enliven flat walls with vibrant texture.

For inspiration, begin your project planning by browsing through the Design Gallery. It's sure to spark your imagination.

Design Gallery

Good interior design doesn't have to be complicated or expensive. And while it's true that many people find it intimidating, it's often merely a matter of confidence. Finding the right elements for your rooms may take some trial-and-error, but keep in mind this essential rule of decorating: if you like it, it's good design.

The following pages will give you some ideas to help get you started. If you look closely, you'll see that most decorating is accomplished using common materials: wallcoverings, moldings, surface textures, paneling, and, of course, paint. Instructions for using all of these materials are included in this book.

(Right) There's no rule that ceilings have to be white. Often the most dramatic changes are made with simple touches, like a coat of paint and wallcovering border.

(Below) A traditional interior can include personal style. In this casual dining room, the bold patterns of the moldings provide a hint of eclecticism, and the simple, brushed color wash of the walls adds a warmth that you don't get with solid paint colors.

©Melabee Miller

©Karen Melvin

(Top) Curves and arches are easier than you may think. This wavy soffit was created with standard framing materials and flexible drywall.

(Above) Glass block adds a new dimension to the meaning of "wall." This bathroom partition separates the functional spaces without blocking light.

(Right) The simplicity of drywall makes it ideal for unusual spaces. In this attic room, the clean lines and smooth finish of the drywalled ceiling accentuate the interesting angles and provide a nice contrast to the wood textures.

©Melabee Miller

©Karen Melvin

(Top) Bold color schemes work best if they're anchored in the room. The bright green walls of this bathroom are reflected in the colors of the sink, vanity top, and mirror frame.

(Above & right) Faux-finishing is a great way to personalize interiors. By combining two or more colors in a basic tone-on-tone finish, you can create a wide range of effects.

©Crandall & Crandall

(Top) With stencils and block printing kits, you can adorn your walls and ceilings with hand-painted details.

(Above) Paint is perfect for highlighting details that might otherwise go unnoticed. This traditional millwork gets new life from a combination of paint colors.

(Left) These walls and ceiling just wouldn't look right with smooth surfaces. Using drywall compound or a texture product, it's easy to replicate the look of plaster or adobe.

A combination of simple elements can add up to a rich interior. The tall baseboard, wallcovering borders, and ceiling panel make this bedroom more intimate.

©Karen Melvin

(Top) Whether on the wall or ceiling, wood paneling adds a great deal of character to a room. Here, knotty-pine beadboard contrasts nicely with a border of classical crown and dentil molding.

(Above) Moldings come in a great variety of styles, and you can combine pieces for custom profiles. This impressive cornice is made up of several types of readily available wood molding.

(Left) Wallcovering is still one of the best tools for creating a formal setting.

Building Walls & Ceilings

Building Partition Walls

Non-load-bearing, or *partition*, walls typically are built with 2 × 4 lumber and are supported by ceiling or floor joists above or by blocking between the joists. For basement walls that sit on bare concrete, use pressure-treated lumber for the bottom plates. As an alternative to wood, you may want to use steel framing to build your walls (see pages 20 to 22).

This project shows you how to build a wall in place, rather than framing a complete wall on the floor and tilting it upright, as in new construction. The build-in-place method allows for variations in floor and ceiling levels and is generally much easier for remodeling projects.

If your wall will include a door or other opening, see pages 18 to 19 before laying out the wall.

A typical partition wall consists of top and bottom plates and 2 × 4 studs spaced 16" on-center. Use 2 × 6 lumber for walls that will hold large plumbing pipes (inset).

> **Everything You Need**
>
> Tools: Chalk line, circular saw, framing square, plumb bob, powder-actuated nailer (for walls in basements), T-bevel (for walls in attics).
>
> Materials: 2 × 4 lumber; blocking lumber; 16d, 10d, and 8d common nails; concrete fasteners (for walls in basements).

Variations for Fastening Top Plates to Joists

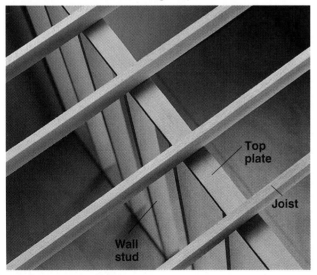

When a new wall is perpendicular to the ceiling or floor joists above, attach the top plate directly to the joists, using 16d nails.

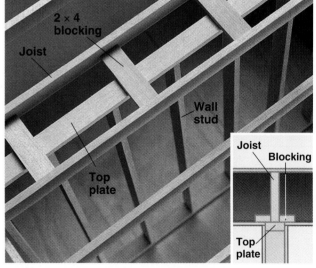

When a new wall falls between parallel joists, fasten the top plate to 2 × 4 blocking installed between the joists every 24". The blocking also provides backing for ceiling drywall. If the new wall is aligned with a joist, install blocks on both sides of the wall (inset).

Variations for Fastening Bottom Plates to Joists

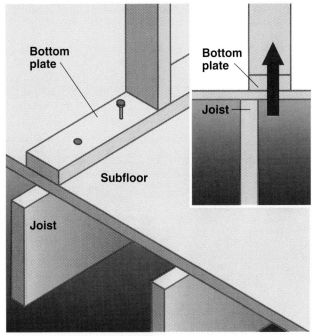

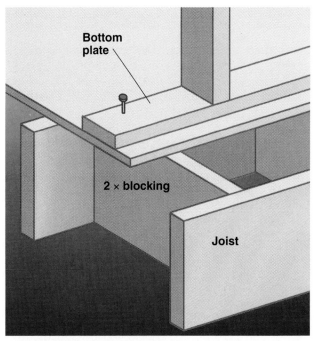

If a new wall is aligned with a joist below, install the bottom plate directly over the joist or off-center over the joist (inset). Off-center placement allows you to nail into the joist but provides room underneath the plate for pipes or wiring to go up into the wall.

If a new wall falls between parallel joists, install 2 × 6 or larger blocking between the two joists below, spaced 24" on-center. Nail the bottom plate through the subfloor and into the blocking.

How to Build a Partition Wall

1 Mark the location of the edge of the new wall's top plate, then snap a chalk line through the marks across the joists or blocks. Use a framing square, or take measurements, to make sure the line is perpendicular to any intersecting walls. Cut the top and bottom plates to length. If the ceiling is finished, mark the joist locations (see page 110).

2 Set the plates together with their ends flush. Measure from the end of one plate and make a mark for the first stud at 15¼", then mark every 16" from there. Thus, the first 4 × 8-ft. drywall panel will cover the first stud and "break" in the center of the fourth stud. Use a square to extend the marks across both plates. Draw an "X" at each stud location.

(continued next page)

3 Position the top plate against the joists, aligning its edge with the chalk line. Attach the plate with two 16d nails driven into each joist. Start at one end, and adjust the plate as you go to keep the edge flush with the chalk line.

4 To position the bottom plate, hang a plumb bob from the side edge of the top plate so the point nearly touches the floor. When it hangs motionless, mark the point's location on the floor. Make plumb markings at each end of the top plate, then snap a chalk line between the marks. Position the bottom plate on the chalk line, and use the plumb bob to align the stud markings between the two plates.

5 Fasten the bottom plate to the floor. On concrete, use a powder-actuated nailer or masonry screws (see page 27), driving a pin or screw every 16". On wood floors, use 16d nails driven into the joists below.

6 Measure between the plates for the length of each stud. Cut each stud so it fits snugly in place but is not so tight that it bows the joists above. If you cut a stud too short, see if it will fit somewhere else down the wall.

7 Install the studs by toenailing them at a 60° angle through the sides of the studs and into the plates. At each end, drive two 8d nails through one side of the stud and one more through the center on the other side.

How to Frame Corners (shown in cutaways)

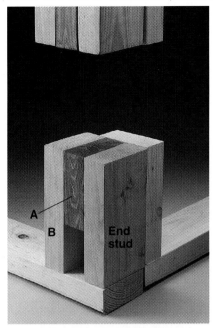

L-corners: Nail 2 × 4 spacers (A) to the inside of the end stud. Nail an extra stud (B) to the spacers. The extra stud provides a surface for attaching drywall.

T-corner meets stud: Fasten 2 × 2 backers (A) to each side of the side-wall stud (B). The backers provide a nailing surface for drywall.

T-corner between studs: Fasten a 1 × 6 backer (A) to the end stud (B) with drywall screws. The backer provides a nailing surface for drywall.

How to Frame an Angled Partition Wall in an Attic

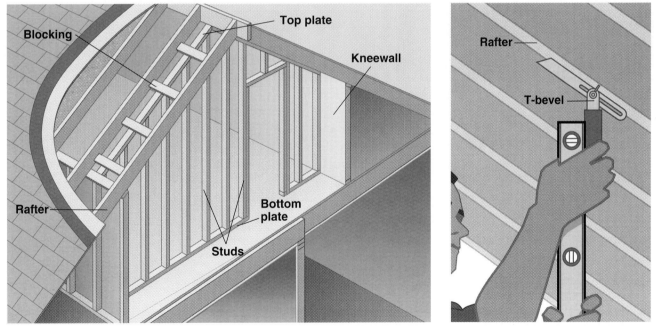

Full-size attic partition walls typically run parallel to the rafters and have sloping top plates that extend down to kneewalls on either side. To build one, cut the top and bottom plates, and mark the stud locations on the bottom plate only. Nail the top plates in place, and use a plumb bob to position the bottom plate, as with a standard wall. Use the plumb bob again to transfer the stud layout marks from the bottom to the top plates. Use a T-bevel and level to find the angle for cutting the top ends of the studs: hold the arm of the bevel plumb and adjust the blade to follow the rafter angle. Transfer the angle to the studs.

How to Frame a Rough Opening for an Interior Prehung Door

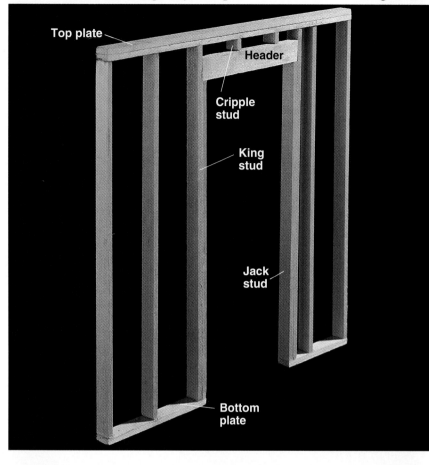

- Top plate
- Header
- Cripple stud
- King stud
- Jack stud
- Bottom plate

Door frames for prehung doors (left) start with *king* studs that attach to the top and bottom plates. Inside the king studs, *jack* studs support the *header* at the top of the opening. *Cripple* studs continue the wall-stud layout above the opening. In non-load-bearing walls, the header may be a 2 × 4 laid flat or a built-up header (below). The dimensions of the framed opening are referred to as the *rough opening*.

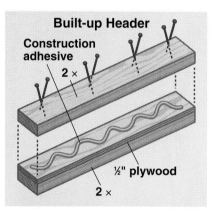

Built-up Header

- Construction adhesive
- 2 ×
- ½" plywood
- 2 ×

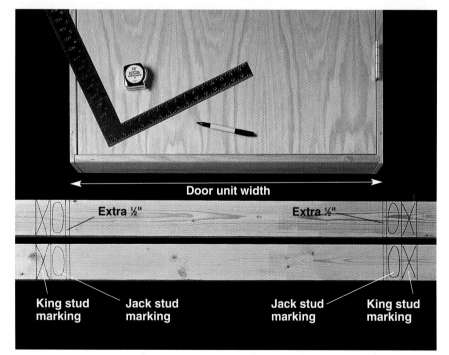

Door unit width

Extra ½" Extra ½"

King stud marking Jack stud marking Jack stud marking King stud marking

1 To mark the layout for the studs that make up the door frame, measure the width of the door unit along the bottom. Add 1" to this dimension to determine the width of the rough opening (the distance between the jack studs). This gives you a ½" gap on each side for adjusting the door frame during installation. Mark the top and bottom plates for the jack and king studs.

2 After you've installed the wall plates (see pages 15 to 16), cut the king studs and toenail them in place at the appropriate markings.

18

3 Measure the full length of the door unit, then add ½" to determine the height of the rough opening. Using that dimension, measure up from the floor and mark the king studs. Cut a 2 × 4 header to fit between the king studs. Position the header flat, with its bottom face at the marks, and secure it to the king studs with 16d nails.

4 Cut and install a cripple stud above the header, centered between the king studs. Install any additional cripples required to maintain the 16" on-center layout of the standard studs in the rest of the wall.

5 Cut the jack studs to fit snugly under the header. Fasten them in place by nailing down through the header, then drive 10d nails through the faces of the jack studs and into the king studs, spaced 16" apart.

6 Saw through the bottom plate so it's flush with the inside faces of the jack studs. Remove the cut-out portion of the plate. NOTE: If you're finishing the wall with drywall, hang the door after the drywall is installed.

Framing with Steel

Steel framing is quickly becoming a popular alternative to wood in residential construction due to the rising cost of wood and the advantages that steel offers. Steel framing is fireproof, insect proof, highly rot-resistant, and lightweight. But the most significant advantage is that steel, unlike lumber, is always perfectly uniform and straight.

Steel studs and tracks (plates) are commonly available at home centers and lumberyards in 1⅝", 2½", and 3⅝" widths. 25-gauge and 20-gauge steel framing is suitable for most non-load-bearing partition walls and soffits that will be drywalled, but 20-gauge results in a somewhat sturdier wall. Use 20-gauge studs for walls that will receive cementboard.

With a few exceptions, the layout and framing methods used for a steel-frame partition wall are the same as those used for a wood-frame wall. For more information on framing partition walls, see pages 14 to 19; for help with framing soffits, see pages 23 to 25.

Here are a few tips for working with steel:

• Steel framing is fastened together with screws, not nails. Attach steel tracks to existing wood framing using long drywall screws.

• Even pressure and slow drill speed make it easy to start screws. Drive the screws down tight, but be careful not to strip the steel. Don't use drill-point screws with 25-gauge steel, which can strip easily.

• Most steel studs have punch-outs for running plumbing and electrical lines through the framing. Cut the studs to length from the same end, to keep the punch-outs lined up.

• The hand-cut edges of steel framing are very sharp; wear heavy gloves when handling them.

• To provide support for electrical receptacle boxes, use boxes with special bracing for steel studs, or fasten boxes to wood framing installed between the studs.

• Use 16"-wide batts for insulating between steel studs. The added width allows for a friction fit, whereas standard batts would slide down.

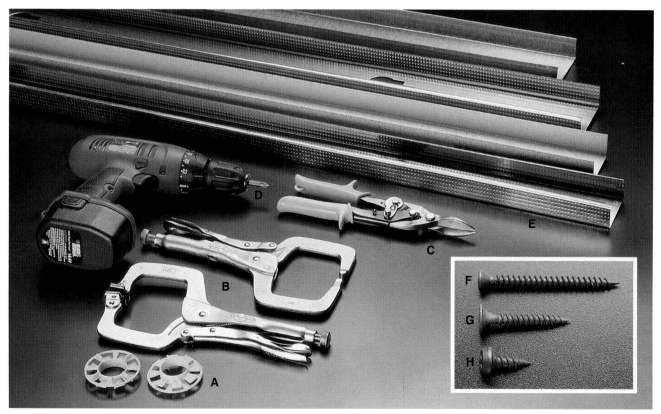

Tools and materials for steel framing include: plastic spacers (A), locking C-clamp pliers (B), aviation snips (C), drill or screwgun (D), and steel track and studs (E). Use self-tapping screws (inset) to fasten steel components. To install wood trim, use type S trim-head screws (F); to fasten drywall, type S drywall screws (G); and to fasten studs and tracks together, ⁷⁄₁₆" type S pan-head screws (H).

Fastening tab

Run electrical and plumbing lines through the stud punch-outs. To prevent galvanic action and electrification of the wall, use plastic spacers when running metal plumbing pipe and electrical cable through studs. Install wood blocking between studs for hanging decorative accessories or wainscoting.

Frame door openings 3" wider and 1½" taller than normal, then wrap the insides with 2 × 4s, providing a nailing surface for hanging the door and installing the casing. Use track for the steel header piece: make fastening tabs by cutting the flanges and bending down the ends at 90°.

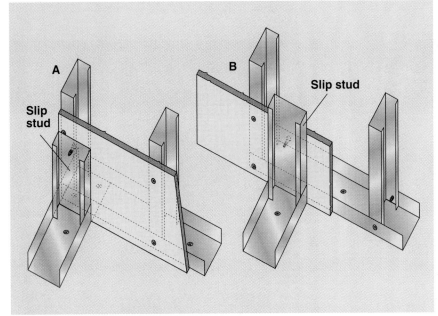

A

Slip stud

B

Slip stud

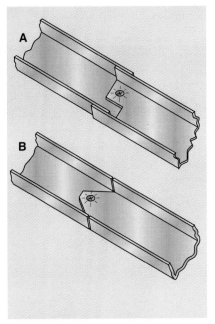

A

B

Build corners using a slip stud: A slip stud is not fastened until the drywall on one wall is in place. Form L-shaped corners (A) by overlapping the tracks. Cut off the flange on one side of one track, removing enough to allow room for the overlapping track and drywall. Form a T-shaped corner (B) by leaving a gap between the tracks for the drywall. Secure each slip stud by screwing through the stud into the tracks of the adjacent wall. Also screw through the back side of the drywall into the slip stud, if possible. Where there's no backing behind the slip stud, drive screws at a 45° angle through the back corners of the slip stud and into the drywall.

Join sections of track with a spliced joint (A) or notched joint (B). Make a spliced joint by cutting a 2" slit in the web of one track. Slip the other track into the slit and secure both with a screw. Make a notched joint by cutting back the flanges of one track and tapering the web so it fits into the other track; secure both with a screw.

How to Frame a Steel Partition Wall

1 Mark the wall location on the floor or ceiling, following the same procedure used for a wood-frame wall. Cut the top and bottom tracks to length with aviation snips. Cut through the side flanges first, then bend the waste piece back and cut across the web. Use a marker to lay out the tracks with 16" on-center spacing (see page 15).

2 Fasten the bottom track to the floor. For wood floors, use 2" coarse-thread drywall screws. For concrete floors, pin the track down with a powder-actuated nailer (see page 27), or use 1¼" masonry screws. Drill pilot holes for screws using a masonry bit. Drive a fastener at each end of the track, then every 24" in between.

3 Plumb up from the bottom track with a plumb bob to position the top track. Fasten the top track to the ceiling joists with 1⅝" drywall screws. Drive two screws at each joist location.

4 Install the studs so the open sides face the same direction (except for door-frame studs). Clamp the stud flange to the track with locking C-clamp pliers and drive a ⁷⁄₁₆" type S pan-head screw through the track into the stud, being careful not to strip it. Drive one screw on each side, at both ends of the stud.

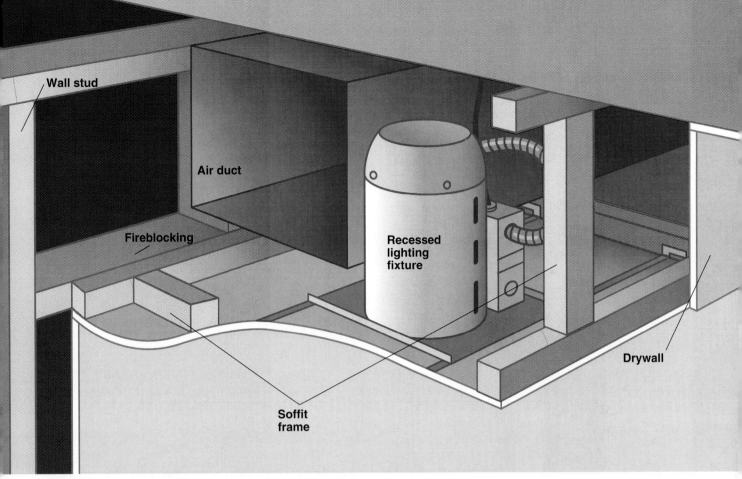

Wall stud

Air duct

Fireblocking

Recessed lighting fixture

Drywall

Soffit frame

Hide immovable obstructions in a soffit built from dimension lumber or steel and covered with drywall or other finish material. An extra-wide soffit is also a great place to install recessed lighting fixtures.

Framing Soffits & Chases

Unfinished basements and other areas often contain elements like beams, pipes, and duct-work, that may be vital to your house but become big obstacles to finishing the space. When you can't conceal the obstructions within walls, and you've determined it's too costly to move them, hide them inside a framed soffit or chase. This can also provide a place to run smaller mechanicals, like wiring and water supply lines.

You can frame a soffit with a variety of materials. 2 × 2 lumber and 1⅝" steel studs both work well, because they're small and lightweight (though steel is usually easier to work with because it's always straight). For large soffits that will house lighting fixtures or other elements, you might want the strength of 2 × 4s or 3⅝" steel studs. Chases should be framed with 2 × 4s or 3⅝" steel studs, so they're as rigid as walls.

The following pages show you some basic techniques for building soffits and chases, but the design of your framing is up to you. For example, you may want to shape your soffits for a decorative effect or build an oversized chase that holds bookshelves. Just make sure the framing conforms to local building codes.

There may be code restrictions about the types of mechanicals that can be grouped together, as well as minimum clearances between the framing and what it encloses. Most codes also specify that soffits, chases, and other framed structures have fireblocking every 10 ft. and at the intersections between soffits and neighboring walls. Remember, too, that drain cleanouts and shutoff valves must be accessible, so you'll need to install access panels at these locations.

Variations for Building Soffits

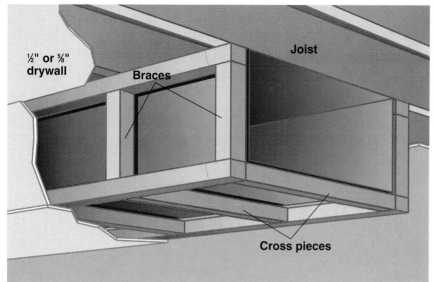

½" or ⅝" drywall

Joist

Braces

Cross pieces

2 × 2 soffit: Build two ladder-like frames for the soffit sides, using standard 2 × 2s. Install braces every 16" or 24" to provide nailing support for the edges of the drywall. Attach the side frames to the joists on either side of the obstruction, using nails or screws. Then, install cross pieces beneath the obstacle, tying the two sides together.

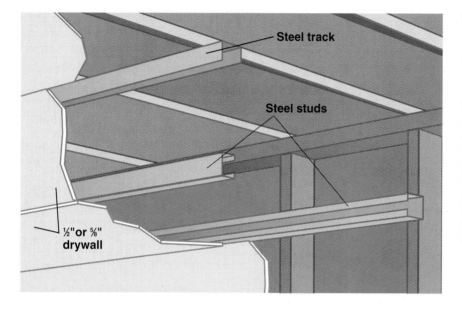

Steel track

Steel studs

½"or ⅝" drywall

Simple steel-frame soffit: With ½" drywall, this construction works for soffits up to 16" wide; with ⅝" drywall, up to 24" wide. Use 1⅝", 2½", or 3⅝" steel studs and tracks (see pages 20 to 22). Fasten a track to the ceiling and a stud to the adjoining wall, using drywall screws. Cut a strip of drywall to form the side of the soffit, and attach a steel stud flush with the bottom edge of the strip, using type S screws. Attach the assembly to the ceiling track, then cut and install drywall panels to form the soffit bottom.

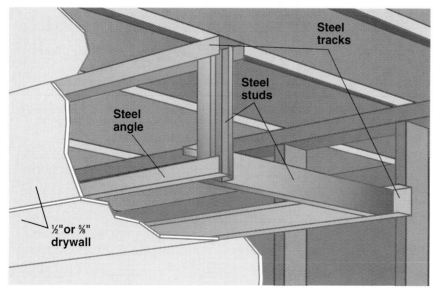

Steel tracks

Steel studs

Steel angle

½"or ⅝" drywall

Steel-frame soffit with braces: Use 1⅝", 2½", or 3⅝" steel studs and tracks. Fasten a track to the ceiling and wall with drywall screws. Cut studs to form the side and bottom of the soffit, fasten them to the tracks every 16" or 24" on-center, using type S pan-head screws, then join the pieces with metal angle (you can use a steel track cut in half lengthwise). Use a string line and locking clamps to help keep the frame straight and square during construction.

How to Frame a Chase

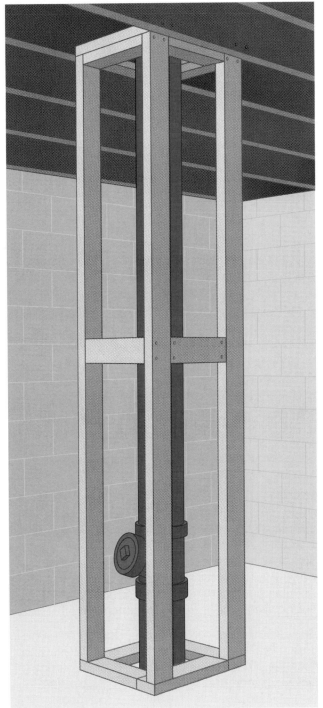

Build chases with 2 × 4s or 3⅝" steel framing. Use steel or pressure-treated lumber for bottom plates on concrete floors, attaching them with construction adhesive and powder-actuated nailer fasteners (see page 27). Add top plates, then install studs to form the corners of the chase. If desired, block in between the studs for stability. To make the chase smaller, notch the top and bottom plates around the obstruction, and install the studs flat. If you're framing around a vertical drain pipe (especially the main DWV stack), leave room around the pipe for soundproofing insulation; plastic pipes can be especially noisy.

Making Access Panels

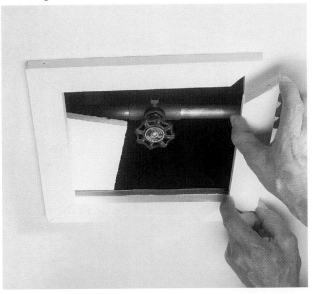

Make access panels after installing drywall. *In a horizontal surface*, cut out a square piece of drywall at the access location, and set it inside the soffit. Glue mitered trim around the opening so it overhangs the edges by ½". Rest the cutout on the trim overhang to cover the opening. *In a vertical surface*, glue the trim to the cutout to create the panel. Install plywood strips to the back of the drywall at two sides of the opening. Secure the panel to the strips with screws.

Attaching Framing to Steel Members

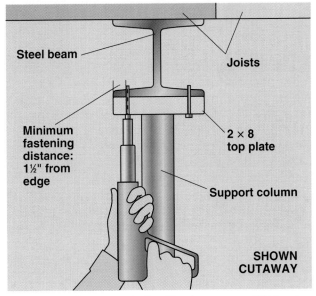

Steel beam

Joists

Minimum
fastening
distance:
1½" from
edge

2 × 8
top plate

Support column

SHOWN CUTAWAY

Use a powder-actuated nailer (see page 27) to attach wood and steel framing to steel I-beams and columns. Hold the nailer at a right angle to the surface and drive the fastener at least 1½" from the edge of the steel. Use a fastener and power load appropriate to the tool and each application. The tool manufacturer should supply a manual, fastener charts, and load charts with the tool. Always wear eye and ear protection when working with these tools.

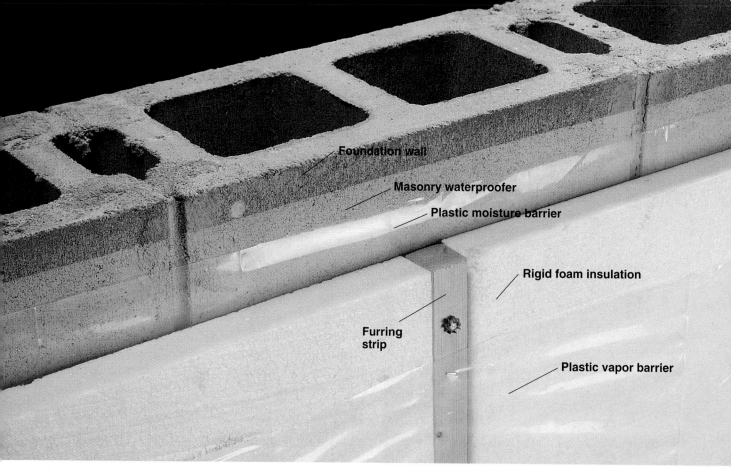

Foundation wall

Masonry waterproofer

Plastic moisture barrier

Rigid foam insulation

Furring strip

Plastic vapor barrier

Local building codes may require a barrier to prevent moisture from damaging wood and insulation covering foundation walls. This may be masonry waterproofer, or plastic sheeting placed behind or in front of the framing.

Covering Foundation Walls

There are two common methods for covering foundation walls. Because it saves space, the more popular method is to attach 2 × 2 furring strips directly to the masonry wall. These strips provide a 1½"-deep cavity between strips for insulation and service lines, as well as a framework for attaching drywall. The other method is to build a complete 2 × 4 stud wall or steel-frame wall just in front of the foundation wall. This method offers a full 3½" for insulation and lines, and it provides a flat, plumb wall surface, regardless of the foundation wall's condition.

To determine the best method for your project, examine the foundation walls. If they're fairly plumb and flat, you can consider furring them. If the walls are wavy or out of plumb, however, it may be easier to build stud walls. Also check with the local building department before you decide on a framing method. There may be codes regarding insulation minimums and methods of running service lines along foundation walls.

A local building official can also tell you what's recommended, or required, in your area for

sealing foundation walls against moisture. Common types of moisture barriers include masonry waterproofers that are applied like paint, and plastic sheeting installed between masonry walls and wood framing. The local building code will also specify whether you need a vapor barrier between the framing and the drywall.

Before you shop for materials, decide how you'll fasten the framing to your foundation walls and floor. The three most common methods are shown on pages 53 to 54. If you're covering a large wall area, it will be worth it to buy or rent a powder-actuated nailer for the job.

Everything You Need

Tools: Circular saw, drill, powder-actuated nailer, plumb bob.

Materials: 2 × 2 and 2 × 4 lumber, 2½" drywall screws, construction adhesive, concrete fasteners, insulation.

Options for Attaching Wood to Masonry

Powder-actuated nailers fasten framing to block, poured concrete, and steel. They use gunpowder caps (*loads*) to drive hardened-steel nails (*pins*). Trigger types (shown) and hammer types are available for sale or rental. NOTE: With block, drive pins into the solid webs, not into the voids.

Masonry nails are the cheapest way to attach wood to concrete block walls. Drive the nails into the mortar joints for maximum holding power and to avoid cracking the blocks. Drill pilot holes through the strips if the nails cause splitting. Masonry nails are difficult to drive into poured concrete.

Self-tapping masonry screws hold well in block or poured concrete, but they must be driven into predrilled holes. Use a hammer drill to drill holes of the same size in both the wood and the concrete, after the wood is positioned. Drive the screws into the block webs, not into the voids.

How to Install Furring Strips on Masonry Walls

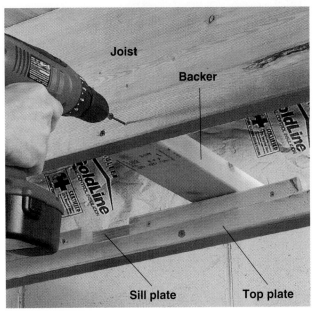

1 Cut a 2 × 2 top plate to span the length of the wall. Mark the furring strip layout onto the bottom edge of the plate, using 16"-on-center spacing (see step 2, page 15). Attach the plate to the bottom of the joists with 2½" drywall screws. The back edge of the plate should line up with the front of the blocks.

Variation: If the joists run parallel to the wall, install backers between the outer joist and the sill plate to provide support for ceiling drywall. Make T-shaped backers from short 2 × 4s and 2 × 2s. Install each so the bottom face of the 2 × 4 is flush with the bottoms of the joists. Attach the top plate to the foundation wall with its top edge flush with the tops of the blocks.

(continued next page)

2 Install the bottom plate cut from pressure-treated 2 × 2 lumber. Apply construction adhesive to the back and bottom of the plate, then attach it to the floor with a nailer or masonry screws. Use a plumb bob to transfer the furring-strip layout marks from the top plate to the bottom plate.

3 Cut 2 × 2 furring strips to fit between the top and bottom plates. Apply construction adhesive to the back of each strip, and position it on the layout marks on the plates. Fasten along the length of each strip every 16".

Variation: Install shorter strips to leave a 2"-wide channel for adding wires or supply pipes. NOTE: Consult local codes to ensure proper installation of electrical or plumbing materials.

4 Fill the cavities between furring strips with rigid insulation board. Cut the pieces so they fit snugly within the framing. If necessary, make cutouts in the insulation to fit around service lines, and cover any channels with metal protector plates before closing up the wall.

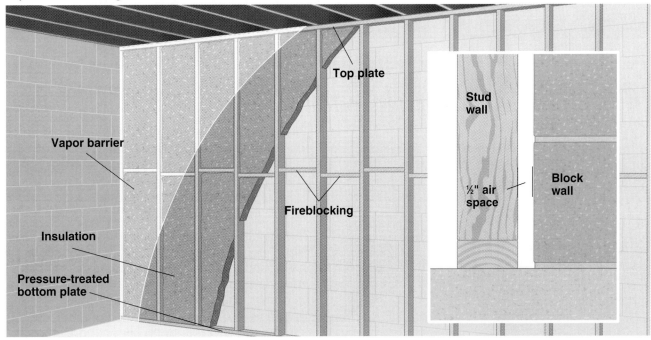

Build a standard partition wall with 2 × 4s or 3⅝" steel framing, following the basic steps on pages 14 to 17 (see pages 20 to 22 for help with steel framing). Use pressure-treated lumber for wood bottom plates that rest on concrete. To minimize moisture problems and avoid unevenness in foundation walls, leave a ½" air space between the stud wall and masonry wall (inset). Insulate the stud wall with fiberglass blankets, and install a vapor barrier and fireblocking if required by local code.

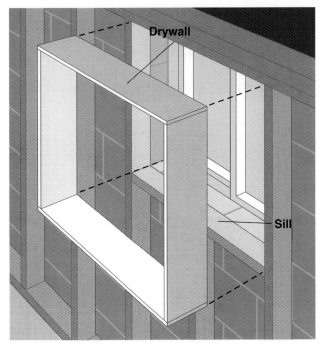

Frame around a basement window so the framing is flush with the edges of the masonry on all sides. Install a sill at the base of the window opening, and add a header, if necessary. Fill the space between the framing members and the masonry with fiberglass insulation or non-expanding foam insulation. Install drywall so it butts against the window frame.

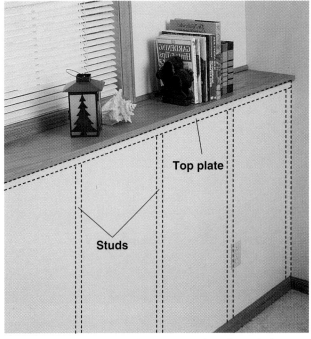

Build a short stud wall to cover a low foundation wall in a walkout or "daylight" basement. Install the top plate flush with the top of the foundation wall. Cover the wall with drywall or other finish, then cap it with finish-grade lumber or plywood to create a decorative shelf.

Framing Curved Walls

Flexible steel track makes it easy to build walls of almost any shape. Tracks come in 10-ft. lengths and fit with 2 × 4s or 3⅝" steel studs.

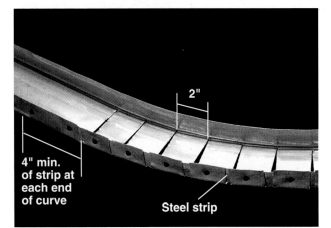

4" min. of strip at each end of curve

2"

Steel strip

As a substitute for flexible track, use standard 20- or 25-gauge steel track. Along the curved portion of the wall, cut the web and flange along the outside of the curve at 2" intervals. From the web of a scrap piece, cut a 1"-wide strip that runs the length of the curve, plus 8". Bend the track to follow the curve, then screw the strip to the inside of the outer flange, using ⅞₆" type S screws. This construction requires 12" of straight (uncut) track at both ends of the curve.

Curved walls have obvious appeal and are surprisingly easy to build. Structurally, a curved wall is very similar to a standard non-load-bearing partition wall, with two key differences: the stud spacing, and the materials used for the top and bottom wall plates.

Traditionally, plates for curved walls were cut from ¾" plywood—a somewhat time-consuming and wasteful process—but now a flexible track product, made of light-gauge steel, has made the construction much easier (see page 140 for supplier information). Using the steel track, frame the wall based on a layout drawn onto the floor. Shape the track to follow the layout, screw together the track pieces to lock-in the shape, then add the studs.

The best stud spacing for your project depends upon the type of finish material you plan to use. If it's drywall, contact the manufacturer to learn the bending properties of their product. Keep in mind that drywall bends more easily when installed with its length perpendicular to the framing (horizontally), rather than parallel. Most drywall manufacturers offer a "flexible" panel designed for curved walls (see page 54). If you will be covering the wall with plywood, space the studs at 2" per foot of outer radius. For example, a wall with a 36" outer radius should have studs spaced 6" on-center.

By virtue of their shape, curved walls provide some of their own stability, so that half-walls with pronounced curves may not need additional support if they're secured at one end. If your wall needs additional support, look for ways to tie it into the existing framing, or install cabinets or other permanent fixtures for stability.

Everything You Need

Tools: Framing square, chalk line, marker, aviation snips, drill, 2-ft. level.

Materials: Flexible metal track, masking tape, ⅞₆" Type S pan-head screws, 2 × 4 lumber, 1¼" coarse-thread drywall screws.

How to Frame a Curved Wall

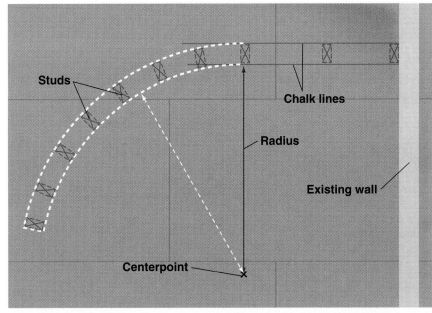

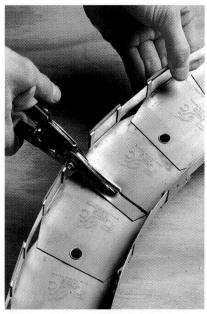

1 Draw the wall layout. Mark straight portions with parallel chalk lines representing the outside edges of the wall track. Use a framing square to make sure the lines are perpendicular to the adjoining wall. At the start of the curve, square off from the chalk line and measure out the distance of the radius to mark the curve's centerpoint. For small curves (4 ft., or so), drive a nail at the centerpoint, hook the end of a tape measure on the nail, and draw the curve using the tape and a pencil as a compass; for larger curves, use a straight board nailed at the centerpoint.

2 Position the track along the layout lines, following the curve exactly. Mark the end of the wall onto the track, using a marker, then cut the track to length with aviation snips. Cut the top track to the same length.

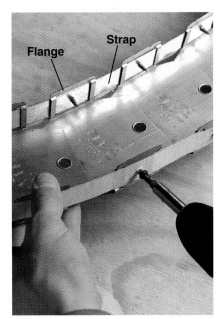

3 Reposition the bottom track on the layout, then apply masking tape along the outside flanges. Secure the track by driving a type S screw through each flange and into the strap. Screw both sides of the track. Set the top track on top of the bottom and match its shape, then tape and screw the top track.

4 Fasten the bottom track to the floor, using 1¼" drywall screws. Mark the stud layout onto both tracks. Cut the studs to length. Install the studs one at a time, using a level to plumb each along its narrow edge, then driving a 1¼" screw through the flange or strap and into the stud on both sides.

5 Fit the top track over the studs and align them with the layout marks. Fasten the studs to the top track with one screw on each side, checking the wall for level and height as you work. Set the level on top of the track, both parallel and perpendicular to the track, before fastening each stud.

Photo Courtesy of Pittsburgh Corning Corporation

Building a Glass Block Wall

With its ability to transmit light, a glass block partition wall defines separate living areas while maintaining a sense of openness. You can find glass block at specialty distributors and home centers in a variety of patterns, shapes, and sizes, along with all the products needed for the installation.

You can build your wall to any height. Top a low wall with a course of bullnose blocks to give it a finished rounded edge, or with flat block to create a shelf. To build a full-height wall, calculate the number of courses of block you'll have, then frame-in a header to fill the remaining space between the finished block and the ceiling.

Follow these tips for a successful installation: When laying out your wall, keep in mind that glass block cannot be cut, so measure carefully. Lay-up the wall using plastic spacers set between the blocks. These ensure consistent mortar joints, and they support the weight of the block to prevent the mortar from squeezing out before it sets. Use premixed glass block mortar, available in dry-mix bags, in white and mortar-gray. When mixing the mortar, follow the manufacturer's directions carefully to achieve the ideal working consistency.

Because of its weight, a glass block wall requires a sturdy foundation. A 4"-thick concrete basement floor should be strong enough, but a wood floor may need to be reinforced (see Tip on page 33). Contact the local building department for requirements in your area. Also bear in mind that glass block products and installation techniques vary by manufacturer—ask a glass block retailer or manufacturer for advice about the best products and methods for your project.

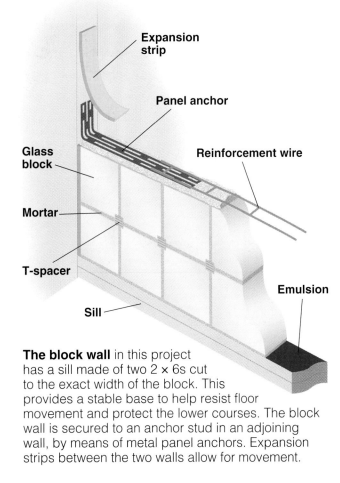

The block wall in this project has a sill made of two 2 × 6s cut to the exact width of the block. This provides a stable base to help resist floor movement and protect the lower courses. The block wall is secured to an anchor stud in an adjoining wall, by means of metal panel anchors. Expansion strips between the two walls allow for movement.

Everything You Need

Tools: Chalk line, circular saw, jig saw, paint-brush, drill, mixing box, trowel, level, pliers, jointing tool, nylon- or natural-bristle brush, sponge.

Materials: 2 × 6 lumber, 16d common nails, water-based asphalt emulsion, panel anchors, 2½" drywall screws, foam expansion strips, glass block mortar, 8" glass blocks, ¼" T-spacers, board, reinforcement wire, 16-gauge wire, caulk or wall trim, baseboard.

32

How to Build a Glass Block Wall

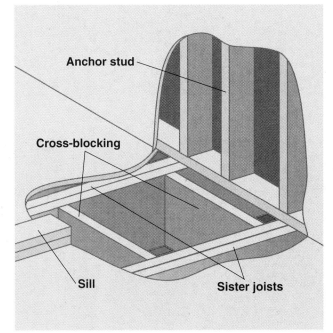

Tip: If necessary, reinforce the floor joists nearest the new wall by installing sister joists and blocking that are the same size as the existing joists. If the new wall is not aligned with an existing wall stud, add an anchor stud centered at the new wall location. You can install the sill directly over the subfloor or over a suitable floorcovering.

1 Dry-lay the first course of glass block, using a ⅜" wood spacer between the wall and the first block, and ¼" spacers between the remaining blocks, to set the gaps for the mortar joints. Mark the wall position onto the floor, then remove the blocks. Snap chalk lines along the marks to create the sill outline.

2 Determine the sill thickness based on the size of your baseboard and thickness of the floorcovering. Rip 2 × 6 lumber to the width of the block. If the end blocks are shaped, trim the sill pieces to match, using a jig saw. Fasten the sill to the subflooring and framing below with 16d common nails. Apply asphalt emulsion to the sill, using a paintbrush.

3 Mark plumb lines on the adjoining wall, straight up from sides of the sill. Mark the finished height of each course along the lines. Fasten a panel anchor to the anchor stud at the top of every second course, using 2½" drywall screws. Cut expansion strips to size and adhere them to the wall between the anchors.

(continued next page)

4 Mix only as much mortar as you can apply in about 30 minutes. Lay a ⅜"-thick mortar bed on the sill, enough for three or four blocks. Set the first block, using ¼" T-spacers at the mortar joint locations (follow the manufacturer's directions for modifying T-spacers at the bottom and sides of the wall). Do not place mortar between blocks and expansion strips. Butter the trailing edge of each subsequent block with enough mortar to fill the sides of both blocks.

5 Lay the remainder of the course. If the wall has a corner, work from both ends toward the center, and install the corner piece last. Use ¼" T-spacers between blocks to maintain proper spacing. Plumb and level each block as you work, then check the entire course, using a flat board and a level. Tap blocks into place using a rubber mallet—do not strike them with a metal tool.

6 At the top of the course, fill the joints with mortar, and then lay a ¼" bed of mortar for the second course. Lay the block for the second course, checking each block for level and plumb as you work.

7 Apply a ⅛" bed of mortar over the second course, then press the panel anchor into the mortar. Repeat this process at each anchor location.

8 Add reinforcement wire in the same joints as the panel anchors, overlapping the anchors by 6". Also overlap the wire by 6" where multiple pieces are needed. At corners, cut the inner rail of the wire, bend the outer rail to follow the corner, then tie the inner rail ends together with 16-gauge wire. Add another ⅛" mortar bed, then lay the next course of block.

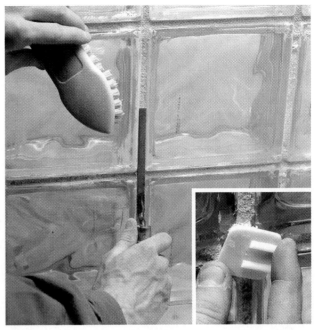

9 Build the wall in complete courses, checking the mortar after each course: when it is hard enough to resist light finger pressure (usually within 30 minutes), twist off the T-spacer tabs (inset) and pack mortar in the voids. Then, tool all of the joints with a jointing tool. Remove excess mortar from the glass, using a brush or damp sponge.

10 Clean the glass block thoroughly, using a wet sponge and rinsing it often. Allow the surface to dry, then remove cloudy residue with a clean, dry cloth. After the mortar has cured for two weeks, apply a sealant. Caulk the seam between the glass block and the adjoining wall, or cover the gap with trim.

11 Reinstall the flooring, if necessary, then cut baseboard to fit around the sill (see pages 106 to 109). If the end of your wall has curved (bullnose) block, wrap the end with three pieces of trim.

Soundproofing Walls & Ceilings

In making homes quieter, building professionals add soundproofing elements to combat everything from the hum of appliances to the roar of airliners. Many of the techniques they use are simple improvements involving common products and materials. What will work best in your home depends upon a few factors, including the types of noises involved, your home's construction, and how much remodeling you have planned. For starters, it helps to know a little of the science behind sound control.

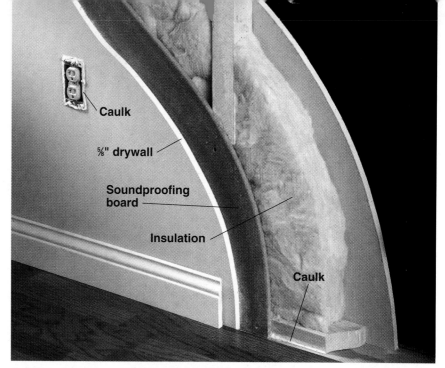

Adding soundproofing board and insulation are among the many simple ways you can reduce noise in your home.

Sound is created by vibrations traveling through air. Consequently, the best ways to reduce sound transmission are by limiting airflow and blocking or absorbing vibrations. Effective soundproofing typically involves a combination of methods.

Stopping airflow—through walls, ceilings, floors, windows, and doors—is essential to any soundproofing effort. (Even a 2-ft.-thick brick wall would not be very soundproof if it had cracks in the mortar.) It's also the simplest way to make minor improvements. Because you're dealing with air, this kind of soundproofing is a lot like weatherizing your home: add weatherstripping and door sweeps, seal air leaks with caulk, install storm doors and windows, etc. The same techniques that keep out the cold also block exterior noise and prevent sound from traveling between rooms.

After reducing airflow, the next level of soundproofing is to improve the sound-blocking qualities of your walls and ceilings. Engineers rate soundproofing performance of wall and ceiling assemblies using a system called Sound Transmission Class, or STC. The higher the STC rating, the more sound is blocked by the assembly. For example, if a wall is rated at 30 to 35 STC, loud speech can be understood through the wall. At 42 STC, loud speech is reduced to a murmur. At 50 STC, loud speech cannot be heard through the wall.

Standard construction methods typically result in a 28 to 32 STC rating, while soundproofed walls and ceilings can carry ratings near 50. To give you an idea of how much soundproofing you

need, a sleeping room at 40 to 50 STC is quiet enough for most people; a reading room is comfortable at 35 to 40 STC. For another gauge, consider the fact that increasing the STC rating of an assembly by 10 reduces the perceived sound levels by 50%. The chart on page 37 lists the STC ratings of several wall and ceiling assemblies.

Improvements to walls and ceilings usually involve increasing the mass, absorbancy, or resiliency of the assembly; often, a combination is best. Adding layers of drywall increases mass, helping a wall resist the vibrational force of sound (⅝" fire-resistant drywall works best because of its greater weight and density). Insulation and soundproofing board absorb sound. Soundproofing board is available through drywall suppliers and manufacturers (see page 140). Some board products are gypsum-based; others are lightweight fiberboard. Installing resilient steel channels over the framing or old surface and adding a new layer of drywall increases mass, while the channels allow the surface to move slightly and absorb vibrations. New walls built with staggered studs and insulation are highly effective at reducing vibration.

In addition to these permanent improvements, you can reduce noise by decorating with soft materials that absorb sound. Rugs and carpet, drapery, fabric wall hangings, and soft furniture help reduce atmospheric noise within a room. Acoustical ceiling tiles effectively absorb and help contain sound within a room but do little to prevent sound from entering the room.

STC Ratings for Various Wall & Ceiling Constructions*

Assembly	STC Rating	Assembly	STC Rating
Wood-frame Walls		**Steel-frame Walls**	
• 2 × 4 wall; ½" drywall on both sides; no caulk	30	• 3⅝" metal studs, spaced 24" on-center; ⅝" fire-resistant drywall on both sides	40
• 2 × 4 wall; ½" drywall on both sides; caulked	35	• 3⅝" metal studs, spaced 24" on-center, ½" fire-resistant drywall single layer on one side, doubled on other side; insulated	48
• 2 × 4 wall; ½" drywall on both sides; additional layer of ⅝" fire-resistant drywall on one side	38	• 2½" metal studs, spaced 24" on-center; soundproofing board (base layer) and ½" fire-resistant drywall on both sides; insulated	50
• 2 × 4 wall; ½" drywall on both sides; additional layer of ⅝" fire-resistant drywall on both sides	40	**Wood-frame Floor/Ceiling**	
• 2 × 4 wall; ½" drywall on both sides; insulated	39	• Drywall below; subfloor and re-silient (vinyl) flooring above	32
• Staggered-stud 2 × 4 wall; ⅝" fire-resistant drywall on each side; insulated	50	• ⅝" fire-resistant drywall attached to resilient steel channels below; subfloor, pad, and carpet above	48
• 2 × 4 wall, soundproofing board (base layer) and ⅝" fire-resistant drywall on each side; insulated	50	• Double layer ⅝" fire-resistant drywall attached to resilient steel channels below; subfloor, pad, and carpet above	Up to 60
• 2 × 4 wall with resilient steel channels on one side; ⅝" fire-resistant drywall on both sides; insulated	52		

*All assemblies are sealed with caulk, except where noted. Ratings are approximate.

Tips for Reducing Exterior Noise

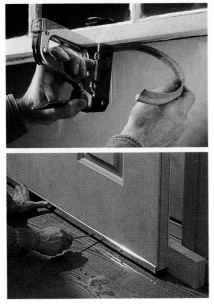

Install weatherstripping on doors and windows to seal off any air leaks. If the wall framing around the door or window is exposed, make sure all cavities are filled with loosely packed insulation.

Add storm doors and windows to minimize air leaks and create an additional sound barrier. Use high-performance (air-tight) storm units and maintain a 2" air gap between the storm and the primary unit.

Seal around pipes, A/C service lines, vents, and other penetrations in exterior walls, using expanding foam or caulk. Make sure through-wall A/C units are well-sealed along their perimeters.

Tips for Reducing Interior Noise

Stop airflow between rooms by sealing the joints where walls meet floors. With finished walls, remove the shoe molding and spray insulating foam, acoustic sealant, or non-hardening caulk under the baseboards. Also seal around door casings. With new walls, seal along the top and bottom plates.

Cover switch and receptacle boxes with foam gaskets to prevent air leaks. Otherwise, seal around the box perimeter with acoustic sealant or caulk and seal around the knockout where the cables enter the box.

Soundproof doors between rooms by adding a sweep at the bottom and weatherstripping along the stops. If doors are hollow-core, replacing them with solid-core units will increase soundproofing performance. Soundproof workshop and utility room doors with a layer of acoustical tiles.

Reduce sound transmission through ductwork by lining ducts with special insulation (see page 140). If a duct supplying a quiet room has a takeoff point close to that of a noisy room, move one or both ducts so their takeoff points are as distant from each other as possible.

How to Install Resilient Steel Channels

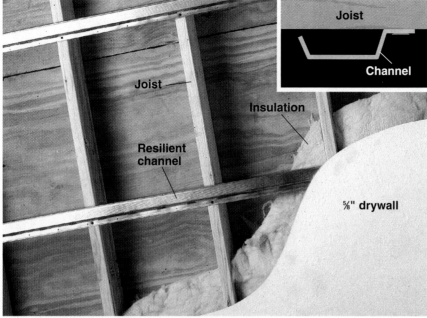

On ceilings, install channels perpendicular to the joists, spaced 24" on-center. Fasten at each joist with 1¼" type W drywall screws, driven through the channel flange. Stop the channels 1" short of all walls. Join pieces on long runs by overlapping the ends and fastening through both pieces. Insulate the joist bays with R-11 unfaced fiberglass or other insulation and install ⅝" fire-resistant drywall, run perpendicular to the channels. For double-layer application, install the second layer of drywall perpendicular to the first.

On walls, use the same installation techniques as with the ceiling application, installing the channels horizontally. Position the bottom channel 2" from the floor and the top channel within 6" of the ceiling. Insulate the stud cavities and install the drywall vertically.

How to Build Staggered-stud Partition Walls

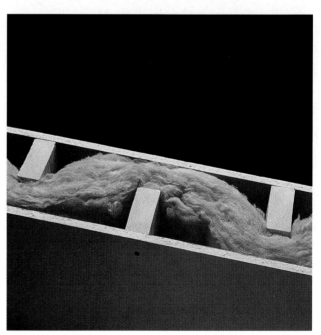

1 Frame new partition walls using 2 × 6 plates. Space the studs 12" apart, staggering them so alternate studs are aligned with opposite sides of the plates. Seal under and above the plates with acoustic sealant.

2 Weave R-11 unfaced fiberglass blanket insulation horizontally between the studs. Cover each side with one or more layers of ⅝" fire-resistant drywall.

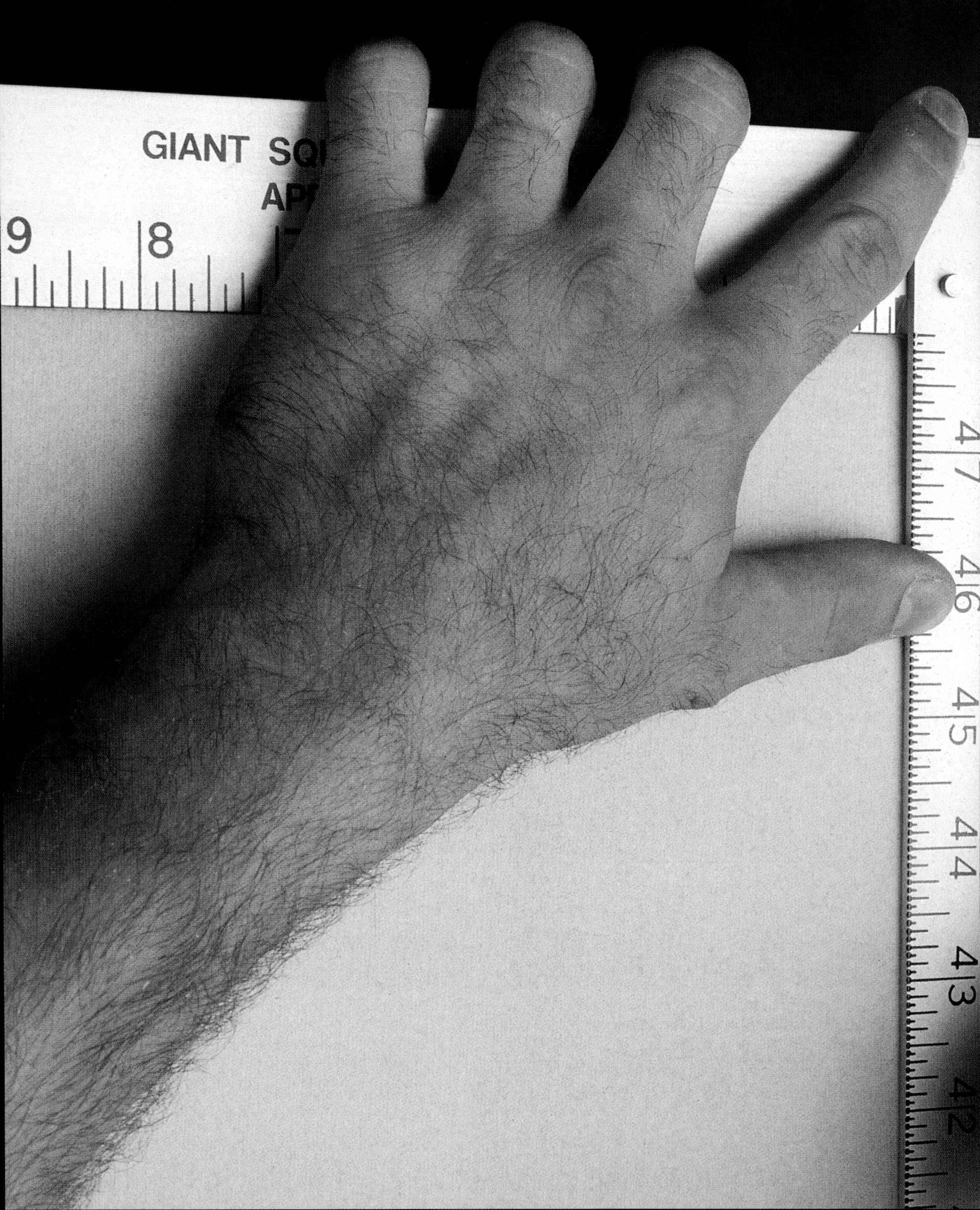
GIANT SQ
AP

Installing & Finishing Drywall

Drywall Basics

Drywall in its present form was developed in 1917 as an economical substitute for plaster. It became popular during the 1940s and today has all but replaced plaster in new construction. Because drywall is inexpensive, perfectly uniform, and easy to install, it's also the best choice for do-it-yourselfers working on remodeling projects.

Drywall panels consist of a core of solid gypsum (a natural mineral product) wrapped in paper. The paper, which is thick, smooth, and white on the panel face and rougher and gray on the back, provides most of the panel's strength, so it's important that the paper remains intact.

The long edges of drywall panels are tapered about 2½" from the edge. When two panels are butted together, the tapered edges create a recess for the joint tape and drywall compound that cover the seam and make the panels appear continuous. The ends of the panels, which are not tapered, are more difficult to finish when butted together.

¼" flexible drywall

⅝" fire-resistant drywall

Moisture-resistant drywall

½" standard drywall

Tapered seam

Drywall Panels

Known by several common names, such as wallboard, gypsum board, and Sheetrock®, drywall comes in a variety of types and sizes, each designed to perform best under specific conditions.

Standard drywall is used for most walls and ceilings in dry, interior areas. It comes in 4-ft.-wide panels in lengths ranging from 8 ft. to 16 ft. and in thicknesses of ¼", ⅜", ½", and ⅝". There are also 54"-wide panels for horizontal installations on walls with 9-ft. ceilings.

Standard ½" panels are appropriate for walls and for ceilings with standard 16" on-center framing. Where ceiling framing is 24" on-center, ⅝" standard panels or ½" *ceiling panels* are recommended to prevent sagging (ceiling panels are specifically designed for this application, and for when heavy, water-based textures will be applied). The ¼" and ⅜" panels are useful for adding a smooth veneer over old, rough surfaces and for curved walls.

Flexible drywall, specially made for curved walls, is a more flexible version of standard ¼"-thick drywall. It can be installed dry or dampened with water to increase its flexibility.

Fire-resistant drywall has a dense, fiber-reinforced core that helps contain fire. Thicknesses are ½", ⅝", and ¾". Your local building department may require fire-resistant panels in garages, on walls adjacent to garages, and in furnace and utility rooms.

Moisture-resistant drywall, commonly called greenboard or blueboard, for the color of its face paper, is made to hold up in areas of high-humidity and against occasional contact with moisture. It is used most often in bathrooms, behind kitchen sinks, and in laundry rooms. For 16" on-center framing, ½"-thick panels are appropriate for walls, and ⅝" panels for ceilings. For wet areas that will receive tile, it's better to use a tile backer (see below) rather than greenboard.

Abuse-resistant drywall withstands surface impacts and resists penetrations better than standard drywall. It's available in ½" regular and ⅝" fire-resistant types.

Foil-backed drywall has a foil layer in its back side that serves as a vapor barrier to prevent interior water vapor from migrating outward into the wall cavity. These panels are not recommended for tile applications or for use in hot, humid climates.

Decorative drywall products are available from various major and specialty manufacturers. Popular options include prefinished vinyl-coated panel systems, decorative corner treatments, prefabricated arches, and drywall panels that look like traditional paneling (right).

Most lumberyards and home centers have ample supplies of common drywall products and tools, but if you can't find what you need, call a drywall supplier, usually listed in the phone book under Building Materials or Drywall.

TILE BACKER

If you're planning to tile new walls in wet areas, such as tub and shower enclosures, use tile backer board as a substrate rather than drywall. Unlike drywall, tile backer won't break down—and ruin the tile job—if water gets behind the tile. There are three basic types of tile backer (see page 140 for supplier information):

Cementboard is made from portland cement and sand reinforced by a continuous outer layer of fiberglass mesh. It's available in ½" and ⅝" thicknesses. See page 55 for installation instructions.

Fiber-cement board is similar to cementboard but is somewhat lighter, with fiber reinforcement integrated throughout the panel material. It comes in ¼" and ½" thicknesses. Cementboard and fiber-cement board cannot be damaged by water, but water can pass through them. To prevent damage to the framing, install a water barrier of 4-mil plastic or 15# building paper behind the backer.

Dens-Shield®, commonly called glass mat, is a water-resistant gypsum board with a waterproof fiberglass facing. Dens-Shield cuts and installs much like standard drywall but requires galvanized screws to prevent corrosion. Because the front surface provides the water barrier, all untaped joints and penetrations must be sealed with caulk before the tile is installed. Do not use a water barrier behind Dens-Shield.

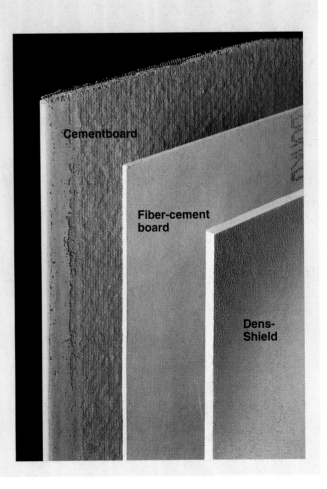

Cementboard

Fiber-cement board

Dens-Shield

Drywall Fasteners

Coarse-thread

Fine-thread

Screws have replaced nails as the fastener-of-choice for most drywall professionals, and for good reason. Screws hold better than nails and are less likely to "pop," they install faster, and they're easier to drive without damaging the drywall. Drywall screws have bugle-shaped heads that help them countersink into the panel surface without breaking the face paper. For wood framing, use coarse-thread screws long enough to penetrate the framing at least ⅝". For steel framing, use fine-thread screws (type S) that penetrate at least ⅜".

Joint Tape

Joint tape is combined with joint compound to create a permanent layer that covers the drywall seams, as well as small holes and gaps. Without tape, thick applications of compound are highly prone to cracking. There are two types of joint tape—paper and self-adhesive fiberglass mesh.

Paper tape comes in 2"-wide rolls. It has a crease down its center, making it easy to fold in half lengthwise for taping inside corners. Paper tape can be used for all taping situations, but because it must be adhered to the wall with joint compound and is somewhat more difficult to use, many drywallers use mesh tape on all tapered seams. Paper tape is stronger than mesh and is the better choice for taping butted seams and inside corners.

Fiberglass mesh tape comes in 2"- and 2½"-wide rolls and has an adhesive backing that sticks to bare drywall. This simplifies the taping coat because you can apply the tape before applying any compound.

Joint Compound

Joint compound, commonly called *mud*, seals and levels all seams, corners, and depressions in a drywall installation. It's also used for some texturing treatments. There are several types of compounds, with important differences among them, but the two main forms are setting-type and drying-type.

Setting-type compound is sold in dry powder form that is mixed with water before application. Because it dries through chemical reaction, setting compound dries quickly (from twenty minutes to six hours, depending on the product)

and is virtually unaffected by humidity and temperature. Setting compounds generally bond better and become harder than drying types, but they're more difficult to sand—characteristics that make them a better choice for the taping coat than for the filler and final coats. Some manufacturers offer lighter-weight setting compounds formulated to be easier to sand.

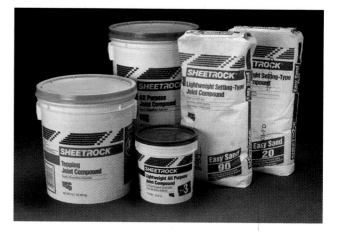

Drying-type compounds dry through evaporation and usually take about 24 hours to dry completely. Available in dry powder and convenient premixed forms, drying compounds are highly workable and consistent. There are three formulas of drying compound: *taping* is a hard-drying formula made for the taping coat; *topping* is somewhat softer and is best for the filler and final coats; and *all-purpose* is a compromise between the other two and is suitable for all coats.

Corner Bead

Corner bead (top photo, facing page) is the angle strip, usually made of metal or plastic, that covers a drywall corner, creating a straight, durable edge where walls intersect. Most corner beads are installed over the drywall and are finished with compound. In addition to standard 90° outside-corner bead, there's an ever-growing variety of bead types designed for specific situations and easy application. There are beads for inside corners, flexible beads for odd angles, J-trims for flat panel edges, bullnose (rounded) beads for inside and outside corners, and a whole range of paper-faced beads that are installed with compound rather than screws.

Drywalling Tools

The basic tools needed for drywalling are shown in the bottom photo on the facing page. Most drywall cuts require a tape measure, a drywall T-square, and a utility knife. A T-square saves time by helping you make straight, square cuts across the entire width of a panel. Use a drywall rasp to smooth cut panel edges,

Bullnose outside corner

Paper-faced inside corner

Paper-faced outside corner

All-metal outside corner

J-trim— unfinished

J-trim— finished

and make holes and other internal cuts with a drywall saw. Cut corner bead with aviation snips.

The best tool for hanging drywall is a screwgun. Similar to a drill, a screwgun has an adjustable nozzle with a clutch device that stops driving the screw at a preset depth. For large jobs, it's practical to rent a screwgun; otherwise, use a variable speed ⅜" drill and drive the screws carefully. A drywall lifter helps you prop up panels while fastening them, but a flat pry bar can perform the same function.

Finishing drywall represents the bulk of the work, but the tools are simple and few. A mud pan holds the compound while you work. It fits nicely into your hand and has sharp edges for

scraping excess mud from the knives. As for knives, the minimum you'll need are a 6" knife for taping and a 12" knife for the filler and final coats—although a 4" taping knife is handy for tight spots, and some drywallers prefer a 10" knife for the filler coat. Don't buy bottom-line or plastic knives, even for a small job, because the money saved won't justify the added frustration.

Sanding completes the job. Professionals use a sanding pole with replaceable fiberglass sanding sheets—a versatile and effective tool, and quite handy for ceilings. Use a sanding pole if your project is large; for small jobs, a dry sanding sponge will be fine.

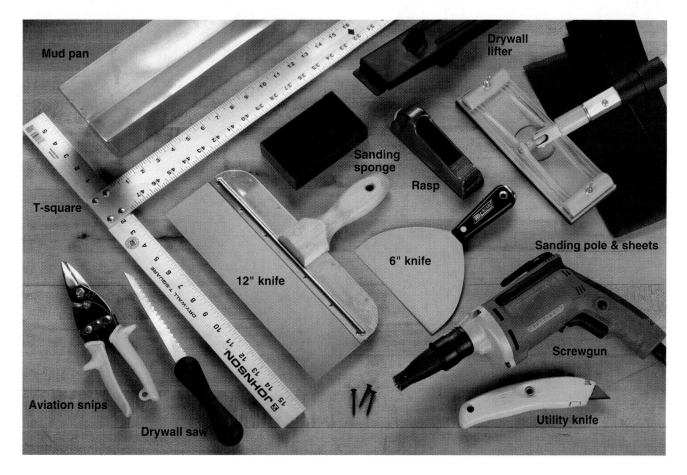

Mud pan

Drywall lifter

Sanding sponge

Rasp

T-square

Sanding pole & sheets

12" knife

6" knife

Aviation snips

Screwgun

Drywall saw

Utility knife

Installing Drywall

Drywall is one of the easiest building materials to install, partly because it allows so much margin for error. Most professional drywallers measure and cut to the nearest ⅛", and it's perfectly acceptable to trim off a little extra from a panel to make it easier to get into a tight space. The exceptions to this are cutouts for electrical boxes and recessed light fixtures, which must be accurate, because the coverplates usually hide less than you think they will.

Begin your installation project by checking the framing—and adding blocking, if necessary—and planning the layout of the panels. Minor flaws in the framing can be hidden by the drywall and mudding, but a severely bowed or twisted stud, or crowned or sagging joists will result in an uneven drywall surface. Follow the tips on page 48 to correct bad studs. For serious joist problems, it's usually easiest to add a grid of furring strips (see page 47). Check the straightness and alignment of the framing using your eye, a level, a straight board, or a string.

Planning the layout will help you reduce waste and deal with problem areas. To save yourself time and trouble during the finishing process, avoid joints where two untapered panel ends are butted together. These are difficult to finish because there's no recess for the mud and tape. In small areas, you can avoid these joints by installing long sheets horizontally that run the full length of the walls. Or you can hang the panels vertically, which produces more seams that need taping but eliminates butted end joints.

If you're installing drywall on both the ceiling and the walls, do the ceiling first, so the wall panels add extra support for the ceiling panels. For large projects, you can arrange to have the drywall delivered, but you'll probably have to unload it yourself. Stack the panels flat until the installation day. When you're ready to hang them, lean the sheets up against a wall with the faces out.

Everything You Need

Tools: T-square, utility knife, drywall saws, drywall rasp, compass, screwgun or drill, drywall lifter, rented drywall lift (for ceilings), chalk line.

Materials: Drywall panels, 1¼" drywall screws.

Additional items for cementboard: Cementboard, 4-mil plastic sheeting, stapler, jig saw, 1¼" cementboard screws, cementboard joint tape, latex-portland cement mortar, drywall taping knife.

Tips for Drywall Preparation

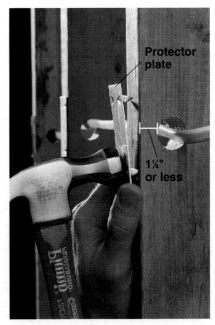

Add backing to support panel edges that won't fall over framing. When installing new panels next to an existing wall surface, or where the framing layout doesn't coincide with the drywall edges, it's often easiest to add an extra stud for backing. See page 27 for adding backing above foundation walls.

Use plywood strips to join panel edges in problem areas between framing, creating a floating seam. This method does not provide a substitute for structural backing; the panels still must be supported by framing or blocking at the prescribed intervals.

Install protector plates where wires or pipes pass through framing members and are less than 1¼" from the front edge. The plates keep drywall screws from puncturing wires or pipes.

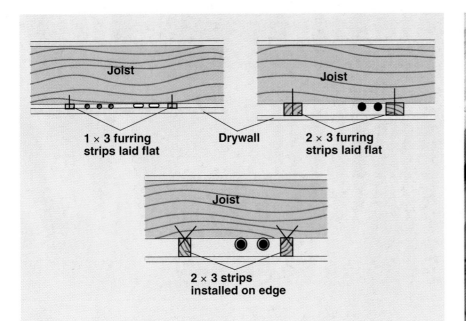

Attach furring strips where service lines and other obstacles project beyond the framing. The strips create a flat surface for attaching drywall and can also be used to compensate for uneven joists. Use 1 × 3 or 2 × 3 furring strips and attach them perpendicularly to the framing with drywall screws. Space the strips 16" on-center and use wood shims secured behind the strips to adjust for unevenness. See page 135 for furring strip installation.

Wrap cold-water pipes along the ceiling with foam insulation before covering them with drywall. This prevents condensation on the pipes that can drip onto the drywall and cause staining.

How to Straighten Bowed Studs

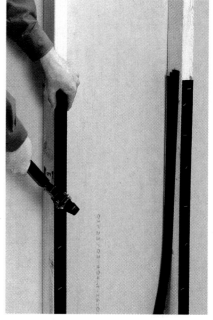

Studs in non-load-bearing walls bowed inward more than ¼" can be straightened. Using a handsaw, make a 2" cut into the stud at the mid-point of the bow. Pull the stud outward, and glue a tapered wood shim into the saw cut to hold the stud straight. Attach a 2-ft.-long 2 × 4 brace to one side of the stud to strengthen it, then trim off the shim. For studs that bow outward, plane down the stud surface with a portable power plane or hand plane. Replace any studs that are severely twisted.

Variation: Staple cardboard strips to stud faces. Use solid strips (not corrugated), which are available from drywall suppliers, or mat board from an art supply store. For extreme bows, start with a 12" to 24" strip and add layers of successively longer strips.

How to Devise a Drywall Layout

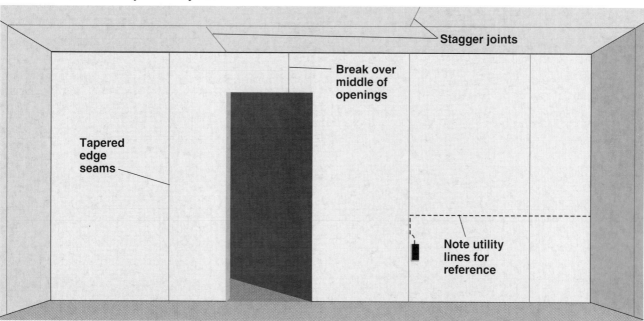

Stagger joints

Break over middle of openings

Tapered edge seams

Note utility lines for reference

Drywall seams must fall on the centers of framing members, so measure the framing when planning your layout. Use long sheets to span an entire wall, or hang sheets vertically. Avoid butted end joints whenever possible; where they do occur, stagger them between rows so they don't fall on the same member. Don't place seams over the corners of doors, windows, and other openings: joints here often crack or cause bulges that interfere with trim. Where framing contains utility lines, draw a map for future reference, noting locations of wiring, pipes, and shutoff valves.

How to Make Straight Cuts in Drywall

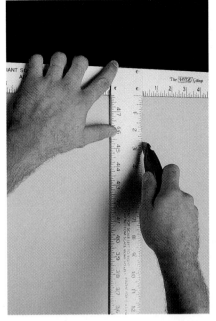

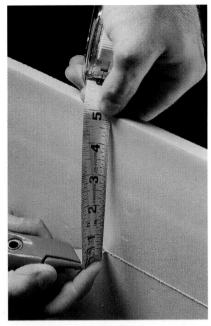

1 To make vertical cuts, set the drywall panel against a wall with the face out. Mark the length on the face, then set a T-square at the mark. Hold the square in place with your hand and foot, and cut through the face paper, using a utility knife.

2 Bend the scored section backward with both hands to break the gypsum core. Fold back the waste piece, and cut through the back paper with the utility knife.

Variation: Make horizontal cuts using a tape measure and utility knife. With one hand, hold the knife blade at the end of the tape. With the other hand, grip the tape at the desired measurement—slide this hand along the panel edge as you make the cut.

3 Smooth rough edges with a drywall rasp. One or two passes with the rasp should be sufficient. To help fit a piece into a tight space, bevel the edge slightly toward the back of the panel.

Tip: Where untapered panel ends will be butted together, bevel-cut the outside edges of each panel at 45°, removing about ⅛" of material. This helps prevent the paper from creating a ridge along the seam. Peel off any loose paper from the edge.

How to Cut Notches in Drywall

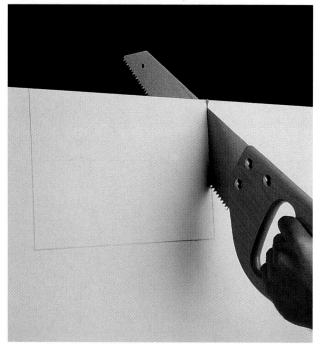

1 Using a large drywall saw, cut the vertical sides of the notch. (These saws are also handy for cutting out door and window openings after the drywall is installed.)

2 Cut the face paper along the bottom of the notch, using a utility knife. Snap the waste piece backward to break the core, then cut through the back paper.

How to Cut Holes in Drywall

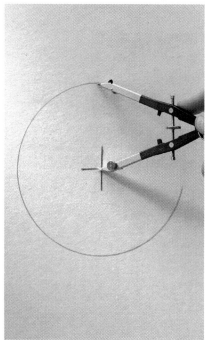

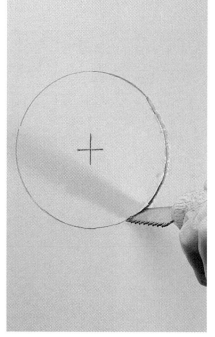

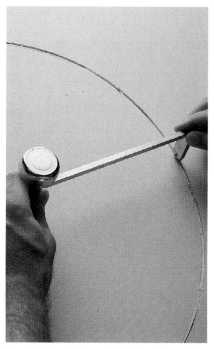

1 To make round cutouts, measure to the center of the object, then transfer the centerpoint to the drywall panel. Use a compass set to ½ the diameter of the cutout to mark the circle on the panel face.

2 Force the pointed end of a drywall saw through the panel from the face side, then saw along the marked line. (These saws work well for all internal cuts.)

Variation: Drive the point of a drywall compass into the center marking, then rotate the compass wheel to cut the face paper. Tap a nail through the centerpoint, score the back paper, then knock out the hole through the face.

How to Cut Drywall with a Router

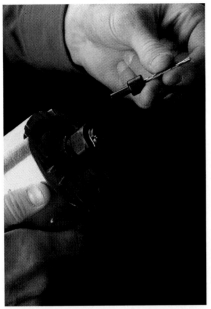

Standard or drywall routers are handy for cutting holes for electrical boxes and openings. You can use a router made for the purpose or outfit a standard router by removing the router base and installing a piloted drywall bit (typically a ¼" shank).

For electrical boxes, mark the floor at the locations of the box centers. Hang the drywall, fastening only at the top edge. Plunge the router bit into the box center, move the bit sideways to the edge, then carefully work the bit to the outside. Follow the outside of the box, cutting counterclockwise.

For doorways and other openings, install the drywall over the opening. Moving clockwise, let the router bit follow the inside of the frame to make the cutout. Always work clockwise when cutting along the inside of a frame; counterclockwise when following the outside of an object, like an electrical box.

Tips for Fastening Drywall

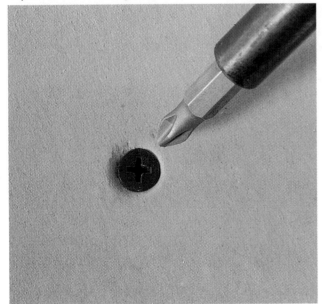

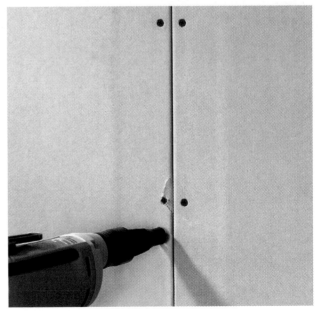

Drywall screws have bugle-shaped heads designed to dimple the panel surface without ripping the face paper. All screws must be recessed to provide a space for the finishing compound. However, driving a screw too far and breaking the paper renders it useless. If this happens, drive another screw about 2" away.

At panel edges, drive fasteners about ½" from the edges. Angle the screw slightly away from the edge, if necessary to prevent breakout. If the fastener tears the paper or crumbles the edge, drive another about 2" away from the first.

How to Install Drywall on Ceilings

1 Snap a chalk line perpendicular to the joists, 48⅛" from the starting wall.

2 Measure to make sure the first panel will break on the center of a joist. If necessary, cut the panel on the end that abuts the side wall so the panel breaks on the next farthest joist. Load the panel onto a rented drywall lift, or use a helper, and lift the panel flat against the joists.

3 Position the panel with the leading edge on the chalk line and the end centered on a joist. Fasten the panel with 1¼" coarse-thread drywall screws driven every 8" along the edges and every 12" in the field.

4 After the first row of panels is installed, begin the next row with a half-panel. This ensures that the butted end joints will be staggered between rows.

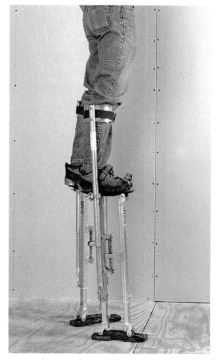

Tip: Drywall stilts bring you within reach of ceilings, so you can fasten and finish the drywall without a ladder. Stilts are commonly available at rental centers and are surprisingly easy to use.

How to Install Drywall on Walls

1 Measure from the wall end or corner to make sure the first panel will break on the center of a stud. If necessary, trim the sheet on the side or end that will be placed in the corner. If you're installing the panels vertically, cut each panel so it's ½" shorter than the ceiling height. Mark the stud centers on the panel face to facilitate fastening.

2 Lift the first panel tight against the ceiling, using a drywall lifter or pry bar, and make sure the side edge is centered on a stud. Fasten the panel with 1¼" coarse-thread screws (for wood framing), driving one every 8" along the edges and every 12" in the field of the panel—don't fasten along the leading edge until the abutting panel is in place.

3 Install the remaining panels, butting the sides together. Avoid placing tapered edges at outside corners, which makes them difficult to finish. If you're running the panels horizontally, set the bottom row tight to the upper row, leaving a ½" gap at the floor. At joints where untapered panel edges are butted, leave a ⅛" gap between panels.

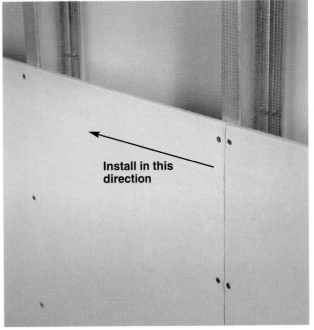

Install in this direction

Variation: When working with steel studs, follow this procedure to avoid uneven seams: install the first sheet from the direction of the open stud faces. Fasten in the field and along the edges completely before installing the adjacent sheet. Where appropriate, drive screws close to the closed edge of each stud. For ½" or ⅝" drywall, use 1" fine-thread screws.

How to Install Drywall on Curved Walls & Arches

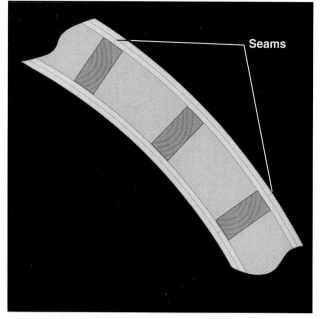

Seams

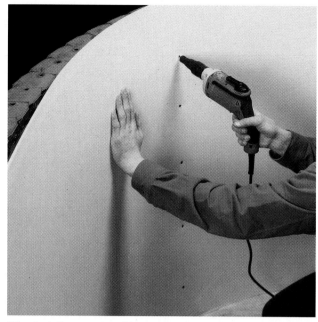

Use two layers of ¼" flexible drywall for curved walls and arches. If the radius of the curve is less than 32", dampen the panels before installing them (see below). The minimum radius for inside (concave) curves is 20"; the minimum for outside (convex) curves is 15". If there are butted seams, stagger the seams between layers. NOTE: Bending limitations may vary by manufacturer.

Start at the center for concave curves. Cut the first panel a little long and position it lengthwise along the wall. Carefully bend the panel toward the midpoint of the curve and fasten it to the center stud. Work toward the ends to fasten the rest of the panel. Install the second panel over the first, then trim along the top of the wall with a drywall saw.

Start at one end for convex curves. Cut the panel long and fasten it lengthwise along the wall, bending the panel as you work. Add the second layer, then trim both to the framing. To cover the top of a curved wall, set a ½" panel on the wall and scribe it from below.

Dampen panels for tight curves. Apply water to the side that will be under tension (the face for convex curves; the back side for concave). Use about 30 oz. of water for a 4 × 8-ft. panel. Stack the panels with their wet sides together, and let them sit for an hour before installing them.

Finish curved edges with flexible vinyl corner bead, which has one segmented flange that allows it to bend. Install the bead as you would standard corner bead (see page 57), but drive a screw every 2". To substitute for flexible bead, snip one flange of standard bead at 1" intervals.

How to Install Cementboard

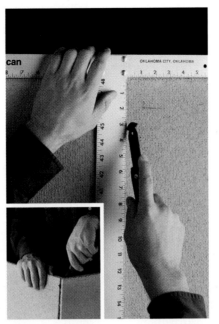

1 Staple a water barrier of 4-mil plastic sheeting or 15# building paper over the framing. Overlap seams by several inches, and leave the sheets long at the perimeter. NOTE: Framing for cementboard must be 16" on-center; steel studs must be 20-gauge.

2 Cut cementboard by scoring through the mesh just below the surface, using a utility knife or carbide-tipped cutter. Snap the panel back, then cut through the back-side mesh (inset). NOTE: For tile applications, the rough face of the board is the front.

Tip: Make cutouts for pipes and other penetrations by drilling a series of holes through the board, using a small masonry bit. Tap the hole out with a hammer or a scrap of pipe. Cut holes along edges with a jig saw and bimetal blade.

3 Install the sheets horizontally. Where possible, use full pieces to avoid cut-and-butted seams, which are difficult to fasten. If there are vertical seams, stagger them between rows. Leave a ⅛" gap between sheets at vertical seams and corners. Use spacers to set the bottom row of panels ¼" above the tub or shower base. Fasten the sheets with 1¼" cementboard screws, driven every 8" for walls and every 6" for ceilings. Drive the screws ½" from the edges to prevent crumbling. If the studs are steel, don't fasten within 1" of the top track.

4 Cover the joints and corners with cementboard joint tape (alkali-resistant fiberglass mesh) and latex-portland cement mortar (thin-set). Apply a layer of mortar with a drywall knife, embed the tape into the mortar, then smooth and level the mortar.

Finishing Drywall

Finishing newly installed drywall is satisfying work that requires patience and some basic skill, but it's easier than most people think. Beginners make their biggest, and most lasting, mistakes by rushing the job and applying too much compound in an attempt to eliminate coats. But even for professionals, drywall finishing involves three steps, and sometimes more, plus the final sanding.

The first step is the *taping* coat, when you tape the seams between the drywall panels. The taping is critical to the success of the entire job, so take your time here, and make sure the tape is smooth and fully adhered before it's allowed to dry. If you're using standard metal corner bead on the outside corners, install it before starting the taping coat; paper-faced beads go on after the tape. The screw heads get covered with compound at the beginning of each coat.

A note on materials: For most jobs, it's easiest to use all-purpose compound for all three coats. To do this, however, you must use paper joint tape rather than self-adhesive mesh tape. Mesh tape is somewhat easier to install than paper, but because it lacks strength, it must be covered in the taping coat with setting-type compound or drying-type taping compound, both of which are stronger than all-purpose (see the discussion of tapes and compounds, on page 44). You can use all-purpose for the other two coats over mesh tape.

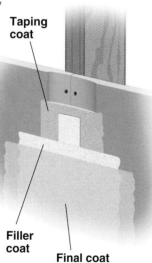

Taping coat

Filler coat

Final coat

After the taping comes the second, or *filler*, coat. This is when you leave the most compound on the wall, filling in the majority of each depression. With the filler coat, the walls start to look pretty good, but they don't have to be perfect; the third coat will take care of minor imperfections. Lightly sand the second coat, then apply the *final* coat. If you're still left with imperfections, add more compound before sanding.

As you work, keep your compound smooth and workable by mixing it in the mud pan frequently, folding it over with the drywall knife. Try to remove dried chunks, and throw away any mud that gets funky or has been added to and scraped off the wall too many times. Always let your compound dry completely between coats. If you have a large ceiling area to finish, it may be practical to rent a pair of drywall stilts (see page 52).

Everything You Need

Tools: Aviation snips, drill, 6" and 12" drywall knives, mud pan, screwdriver, sanding pole or hand sander, sanding sponge, utility knife.

Materials: Corner bead, 1¼" drywall screws, joint compound, joint tape, 220-grit sanding screen or 150-grit sandpaper, light.

How to Install Corner Bead

1 Cut metal corner bead to length so there will be a ½" gap at the floor, using aviation snips. Position the bead so the raised spine is centered over the corner and the flanges are flat against both walls.

2 Starting at the top, fasten the bead flanges with 1¼" drywall screws, driven every 9" and about ¼" from the edge. Alternate sides with each screw to keep the bead centered. The screws must not project beyond the raised spine.

How to Apply the Taping Coat

1 Inspect the entire drywall installation and fill any gaps wider than ¼" with compound. Smooth off excess compound so it's flush with the panel face. Also remove any loose paper from damaged areas and fill in with compound.

2 Cover all screw heads with compound. Using a 4" or 6" taping knife, smear compound over the screw head, forcing it into the depression. Firmly drag the knife in the opposite direction, removing excess compound from the panel surface. Use a screwdriver to drive any protruding screws.

(continued next page)

3 On tapered seams, apply an even bed layer of compound over the seam, about ⅛" thick and 6" wide, using a 6" taping knife. For paper tape, use a setting-type, premixed taping, or all-purpose compound. Use paper tape on all butted end joints.

4 Center the tape over the seam and lightly embed it in the compound, making sure the tape is smooth and straight. At the end of the seam, tear off the tape so it extends all the way into inside corners and up to the corner bead at outside corners.

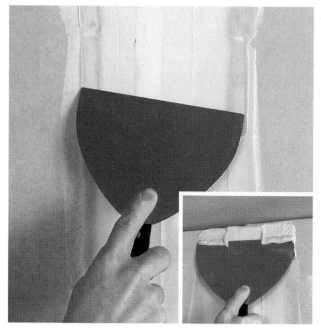

5 Smooth the tape with the taping knife, working out from the center. Apply enough pressure to force compound from underneath the tape, so the tape is flat and has a thin layer beneath it. At inside corners, smooth the final bit of tape by reversing the knife and carefully pushing it toward the corner (inset). Remove excess compound along the edges of the bed layer.

Variation: To use self-adhesive mesh tape on seams, apply the tape over the seam center so it's straight and flat. Coat the tape with an even layer of compound, about ⅛" thick, using a 6" taping knife. Smooth the joint with a 10" or 12" knife, removing excess compound so that only the recessed seam is covered.

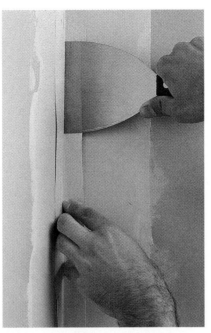

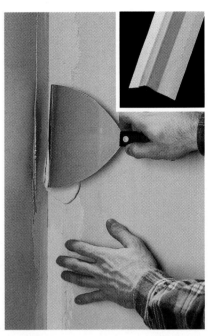

6 Tape inside corners by folding precreased paper tape in half to create a 90° angle. Apply an even layer of compound, about ⅛" thick and 4" wide, to both sides of the corner, using a 4" or 6" knife.

7 Embed the tape into the compound, using your fingers and the knife. Carefully smooth and flatten both sides of the tape, removing excess compound to leave only a thin layer beneath. Make sure the center is straight.

Variation: Paper-faced metal inside corner bead produces straight, durable corners with little fuss. To install the bead, embed it into a thin layer of compound, then smooth the paper, as with a paper-tape inside corner.

8 Finish outside corner bead with a 6" knife. Apply the compound while dragging the knife along the raised spine of the bead. Make a second pass to feather the outside edge of the compound, then a third dragging along the bead again. Smooth any areas where the corner bead meets taped corners or seams.

Variation: To install paper-faced outside corner bead, spread an even layer of compound on each side of the corner, using a 6" taping knife. Press the bead into the compound and smooth the paper flanges with the knife.

How to Apply the Filler Coat

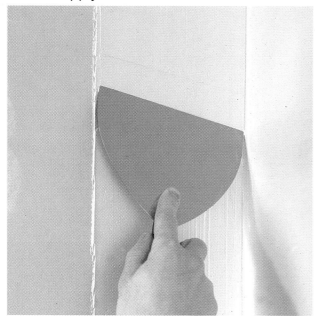

1 Scrape off ridges and chunks left from the taping coat, then second-coat the screw heads (see page 57). Apply an even layer of compound to both sides of each inside corner, using a 6" knife. Smooth one side at a time, holding the blade about 15° from horizontal and lightly dragging the point along the corner. Make a second pass to remove excess compound along the outer edges. Repeat, if necessary.

2 Second-coat the outside corners, one side at a time, using a 12" knife. Apply an even layer of compound, then feather the outside edge by applying pressure to the outside of the knife—enough so that the blade flexes and removes most of the compound along the edge but leaves the corner intact. Make a second pass with the blade riding along the raised spine, applying even pressure.

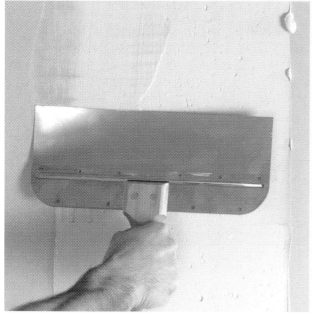

3 Coat flat (tapered or end-butted) seams with an even layer of compound, using the 12" knife. Whenever possible, apply the coat in one direction and smooth it in the opposite. Feather the sides of the compound first, holding the blade almost flat and applying pressure to the outside of the blade so the blade just skims over the center of the seam.

4 After feathering both side edges of the compound, make a pass down the center of the seam, applying even pressure to the blade. This pass should leave the seam smooth and even, with the edges feathered out to nothing. The joint tape should be completely covered.

How to Apply the Final Coat

1 After the filler coat has dried, lightly sand all of the joints (see page 62), then third-coat the screws. Apply the final coat, following the same steps used for the filler coat but do the seams first, then the outside corners, followed by the inside corners. Use a 12" knife and spread the compound a few inches wider than the joints in the filler coat. Remove most of the compound, filling scratches and low spots but leaving only traces elsewhere. Make several passes, if necessary, until the surface is smooth and there are no knife tracks or other imperfections. Carefully blend intersecting joints so there's no visible transition.

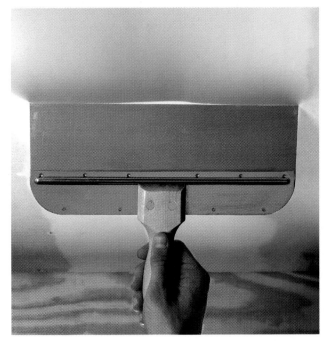

2 Inspect the entire job for flaws after the final coat has dried. To check seams, hold a level or 12" knife perpendicularly across the seam: fill concave seams with an extra layer or two or compound, repeating the filler and final coats. Correct any convex seams that are crowned more than $\frac{1}{16}$" (see step 3).

3 Correct crowned seams by sanding carefully along the seam's center (see page 62), but do not expose the joint tape. Check the joint with a level. If it's still crowned, add a layer of compound about 24" wide. Smooth the compound with a 12" knife, removing all of it along the seam's center and feathering it out toward the outside edges. After that coat dries, apply a final coat, if necessary.

How to Flat Tape

1 Trim any loose paper along the drywall edge with a utility knife. If the gap between the drywall and the object is wider than ¼", fill it with joint compound and let it dry. Cover the joint with self-adhesive mesh joint tape, butting the tape's edge against the object without overlapping the object.

2 Cover the tape with a 4"-wide layer of setting-type or premixed taping compound. Smooth the joint, leaving just enough compound to conceal the tape. Let the first coat dry completely, then add two more thin coats, using a 6" taping knife. Feather the outside edge of the joint to nothing.

How to Sand Drywall

1 Lightly sand all joints, using a hand or pole sander with 220-grit sanding screen or 150-grit sandpaper. Work in the direction of the joints, smoothing transitions and high areas. Don't sand out depressions; fill them with compound and resand. Be careful not to oversand or expose joint tape.

2 To avoid damage or oversanding, use a 150-grit sanding sponge to sand inside corners. Fine-sand the seams and screws with a sponge or hand sander, feeling for defects with your hand. Use a bright light to highlight problem areas. Remove dust from the panels with dry towel or soft broom.

Variation: Wet sanding is a dust-free alternative to dry sanding. Use a high-density, small-cell polyurethane sponge made for wet sanding. Saturate the sponge with cool, clean water, and wring it out just enough so it doesn't drip. Swipe joints and corners in the direction they run, and rinse the sponge frequently. Sponge as little as possible, to avoid streaking.

Repairing Drywall

Most drywall problems can be remedied with basic drywalling materials: screws, joint tape, drywall, joint compound, and corner bead. To repair holes left by nails or screws, dimple the hole slightly with the handle of a utility knife or drywall knife and fill it with spackling or drywall compound.

For doorknob-sized holes or gaps created by inaccurate cutouts, use self-adhesive mesh joint tape covered with three coats of joint compound. Also use joint tape anywhere the face paper has been torn or peeled away. Repair larger holes with a patch of drywall.

Resetting popped fasteners is another common repair. Caused by shrinkage in wood framing or improperly fastened panels, popped fasteners appear as round protrusions or exposed screw or nail heads.

See pages 56 to 62 for help with drywall finishing products and techniques. Lightly sand your repairs before painting, or add a texture (pages 66 to 69).

Everything You Need

Tools: Drill or screwgun, hammer, 6" and 12" drywall knives, framing square, drywall saw, hacksaw, file.

Materials: 1¼" drywall screws, drywall joint compound, 150-grit sandpaper, wood scraps, self-adhesive mesh joint tape.

How to Reset Popped Fasteners

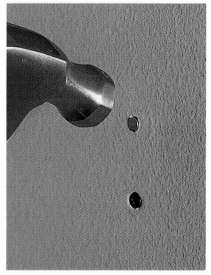

1 Press the drywall panel tight against the framing, then drive a screw about 2" from the popped fastener. Recess the screw head slightly without breaking the panel's face paper.

2 Hammer in, or screw in, the popped fastener, leaving a slight indentation. Fill both depressions with two coats of drywall compound, then sand and repaint.

How to Patch Small Holes

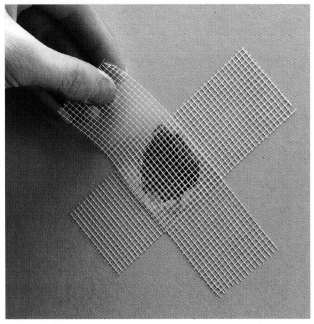

Fill shallow depressions and scratches with two or more coats of drywall compound. For small holes, cover the area with crossed strips of self-adhesive mesh joint tape. Cover the tape with compound, lightly forcing it into the mesh, then smooth it off, leaving just enough to conceal the tape. Add two more coats, in successively broader and thinner coats, to blend the patch into the surrounding area.

Patch gaps around electrical boxes and other fixtures when coverplates are too small to hide the defect. Fill the gap with drywall compound, then cover it with mesh joint tape. Smooth off excess compound and let the patch dry. Add two more thin layers of compound to cover the tape and blend the patch into the surrounding area.

How to Patch Large Holes

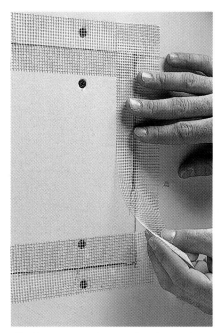

1 Outline the damaged area, using a framing square. (Cutting four right angles makes it easier to measure and cut the patch.) Use a drywall saw to cut along the outline.

2 Cut plywood or lumber backer strips a few inches longer than the height of the cutout. Fasten the strips to the back side of the drywall, using 1¼" drywall screws.

3 Cut a drywall patch ⅛" smaller than the cutout dimensions, and fasten it to the backer strips with screws. Apply mesh joint tape over the seams. Finish the seams with three coats of compound.

How to Repair Metal Corner Bead

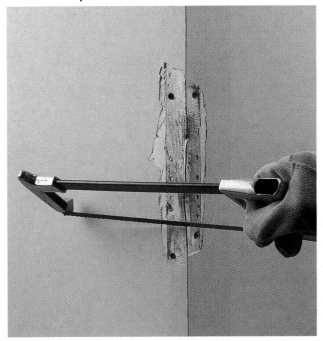

1 Drive a 1¼" drywall screw into each flange of the metal corner bead, above and below the damaged area. Cut out the damaged section of corner bead, using a hack saw. Cut through the raised spine first, then the flanges, keeping the saw blade parallel to the floor. Remove the damaged section, and scrape away any loose drywall and compound.

2 Cut a new piece of corner bead to fit exactly into the opening. Hold the replacement piece so the spine is perfectly aligned with the existing corner piece and secure it with drywall screws. Drive the screws about ¼" from the flange edge, and alternate sides with each screw to keep the piece straight.

3 File the seams with a fine metal file to ensure a smooth transition between pieces. If you can't easily smooth the seams, cut a new replacement piece and start over.

4 Hide the repair with three coats of drywall compound.

Texturing Walls & Ceilings

Wall and ceiling textures can take almost any form, and today's texturing products make it easy to create a range of effects—from acoustical spray textures to custom hand-troweled designs.

Most textures are applied using hand tools, such as paint rollers and drywall knives, or pneumatic texturing guns, which you can find at rental centers. Spray equipment is not difficult to use, but make sure to get operating instructions or a lesson at the rental center. If you are hand-applying a texture on a ceiling, you may want to rent a pair of drywall stilts (see page 52).

Home centers and paint stores carry a wide variety of do-it-yourself texturing products. One of the easiest to use is texture paint, because it combines a paint base (usually white) with texture additives and doesn't need to be painted after it's applied. You can also buy dry additives separately and mix them into the paint of your choice. For many texture treatments, you can also use all-purpose drywall compound, thinning it with water, if desired. Textures made with compound must be painted, however.

Texture products typically contain a lot of water and can be heavy if applied in thick coats. Drywalled ceilings that receive a popcorn texture or heavy coats of compound must be adequately supported to resist sagging. Standard ½" drywall panels should be attached to joists that are 16" on-center. Where framing is 24" on-center, the drywall should be ⅝" standard or ½" ceiling panels (see page 42). Texturing is not recommended on ceilings with ⅜" drywall.

Before texturing, prepare new walls and ceilings with a coat of flat, white latex wall paint (or use a base-coat product made specifically for texturing). If you're texturing old surfaces, consult the manufacturer regarding prep work. To ensure consistent drying, texture when the air temperature, the wall or ceiling surface, and the texture material are at least 55°F. Ventilate the room only after application, and don't use heaters to speed the drying process.

How to Apply a Popcorn Ceiling Texture

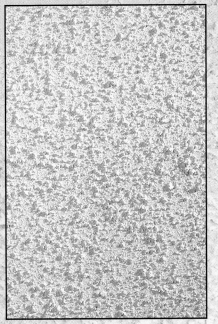

Popcorn texture is a popular treatment for ceilings. Its bumpy surface is created by tiny particles of vermiculite or polystyrene that give it sound-deadening properties. Mixtures are available in fine, medium, and coarse grades.

Mix the dry texture following the manufacturer's directions, and load the hopper of the texture gun. Apply the texture, holding the gun 2 ft. to 4 ft. below the ceiling. Spray in a side-to-side motion (not arching), leaving a thin, even layer over the entire ceiling. Immediately following the first layer, spray on a second thin layer, working in a direction perpendicular to the first. Allow the texture to dry. For a heavy texture, the manufacturer may recommend applying an additional coat.

How to Apply an Orange Peel Texture

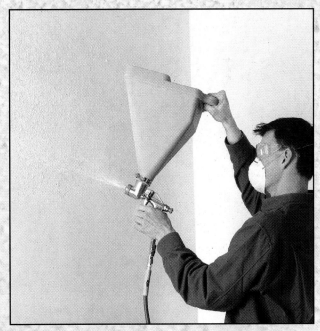

Orange peel textures are most commonly applied to walls. They have a distinctive, spattered look created by spraying a thin texturing product or water-thinned all-purpose drywall compound through a texturing gun. For a heavier spattered texture, repeat the step shown here, using less air pressure at the gun (atomizing air) and the compressor (feed pressure).

Mix the texture product or compound to the consistency of latex paint. Spray the surface with long, side-to-side strokes, keeping the gun perpendicular to the surface, and about 18" away from it. To apply a heavy spatter-coat, let the surface dry for 10 to 15 minutes, then spray with random motions, from about 6 ft. away.

How to Create a Knock-down Texture

A knock-down texture is an orange peel texture that is partially smoothed with a drywall knife. Its relative flatness creates a subtle effect, and it's easier to paint and maintain than the heavier textures, making it a good choice for walls. Because of the light troweling required, this texture works best on smooth, flat surfaces.

Mix the texture product or all-purpose drywall compound to a heavy latex-paint consistency. Spray-texture the entire surface following the orange peel procedure on page 67. Let the texture dry for 10 to 15 minutes, then lightly trowel the surface with a 12" or larger drywall knife. Hold the knife almost flat, and work perpendicularly to the drywall seams.

How to Apply a Stipple Texture

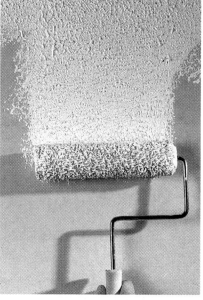

Stipple textures are made with a paint roller and texture paint or all-purpose drywall compound. Randomly shaped ridges have a noticeable grain orientation. The amount of texture is affected by the nap of the roller, which can vary from ¼" to 1". Stippling can be knocked down for a flatter finish.

Mix paint or compound to a heavy latex-paint consistency. Coat the roller and roll the surface, recoating the roller as needed to create an even layer over the entire work area. Let the texture dry to a dull-wet sheen, then roll the surface again—without loading the roller—to create the finished texture.

Variation: Knock down the stipple finish for a smoother texture. Apply the stipple texture with a roller, and let it dry for about 10 minutes. Smooth the surface with a 12" or larger drywall knife, holding the knife almost flat and applying very light pressure.

How to Create a Swirl Texture

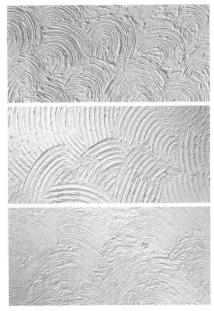

Swirl textures and other freehand designs can have the look of traditionally applied plaster. Swirls can be made with a wallpaper brush, wisk broom, or any type of raking or combing tool.

Mix the texture product or all-purpose drywall compound to a heavy latex-paint consistency. For a shallow texture, use a paint roller with a ½" nap to apply an even coat over the entire surface; for a deeper texture, apply an even, ⅛"-thick coat with a drywall knife. Let the surface dry to a dull-wet appearance. Brush the pattern into the material using arching or circular motions. Start at one end of the area and work backward, overlapping the starting and end points of previous swirls with each new row.

How to Apply a Troweled Texture

A troweled texture can have almost any design but should be applied with varied motions to create a random appearance. Premixed all-purpose drywall compound works well for most troweled textures, and it's usually best to work in small sections.

1 Apply the compound to the surface using a 6" or 8" drywall knife. Vary the direction of the strokes and the thickness of compound. If desired, stipple the surface by stamping the knife into the compound and pulling it away sharply.

2 Partially smooth the surface, using a 6", 8", or 12" knife. Flatten the tops of ridges and stipples without smoothing lower areas. When you're satisfied with the design, repeat step 1 in an adjacent section, overlapping the edges of the textured area by a few inches.

Finishing Walls & Ceilings

©Karen Melvin

Basic Painting

Paints are either latex (water-based) or alkyd (oil-based). Latex paint is easy to apply and clean up, and the improved chemistry of today's latexes makes them suitable for nearly every application. Some painters feel that alkyd paint provides a smoother finish, but local regulations may restrict the use of alkyd products.

Paints come in various sheens. Paint finishes range from high-gloss to flat enamels. Gloss enamels dry to a shiny finish and are used for surfaces that need to be washed often, such as walls in bathrooms and kitchens, and woodwork. Flat paints are used for most wall and ceiling applications.

Paint prices typically are an accurate reflection of quality. As a general rule, buy the best paint your budget can afford. High-quality paints are easier to use, and they look better than cheaper paints. Quality paints last longer and cover better than budget paints, and because they often require fewer coats, they are usually less expensive in the long run.

Before applying the finish paint, prime all of the surfaces with a good-quality primer. Primer bonds well to all surfaces and provides a durable base that keeps the paint from cracking and peeling. Priming is particularly important when using a high-gloss paint on walls and ceilings, because the paint alone might not completely hide finished drywall joints and other variations in the surface. To avoid the need for additional coats of expensive finish paint, tint the primer to match the new color.

How to Estimate Paint

1) Length of wall or ceiling (linear feet)	
2) Height of wall, or width of ceiling	×
3) Surface area (square feet)	=
4) Coverage per gallon of chosen paint	÷
5) Gallons of paint needed	=

Tips for Selecting Paint

Paint comes in a variety of surface finishes, or *sheens*. Gloss enamel (A) provides a highly reflective finish for areas where washability is important. All gloss paints tend to show surface flaws. Alkyd enamels have the highest gloss. Medium-gloss latex enamel creates a highly washable surface with a slightly less reflective finish. Like gloss enamels, medium-gloss paints (B) tend to show surface flaws. Eggshell enamel (C) combines a softer finish with the washability of enamel. Flat latex (D) is an all-purpose paint with a soft finish that hides surface irregularities.

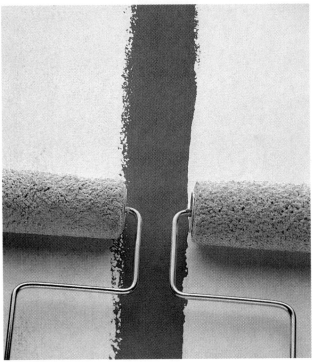

Paint coverage (listed on can labels) of quality paint should be about 400 square feet per gallon. Bargain paints (left) may require two or even three coats to cover the same area as quality paints.

High washability is a feature of quality paint. The pigments in bargain paints (right) may "chalk" and wash away with mild scrubbing.

Painting Tools

Most painting jobs can be completed with a few quality tools. Purchase two or three premium brushes, a sturdy paint pan that can be attached to a stepladder, and one or two good rollers. With proper cleanup, these tools will last for years. See pages 76 to 77 for tips on how to use paintbrushes and rollers.

Tips for Choosing a Paintbrush

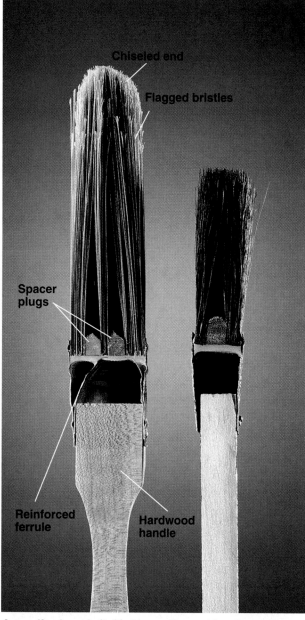

A quality brush (left), has a shaped hardwood handle and a sturdy, reinforced ferrule made of noncorrosive metal. Multiple spacer plugs separate the bristles. A quality brush has flagged (split) bristles and a chiseled end for precise edging. A cheaper brush (right) will have a blunt end, unflagged bristles, and a cardboard spacer plug that may soften when wet.

There's a proper brush for every job. A 3" straight-edged brush (top) is good for cutting in along ceilings and corners. For woodwork, a 2" trim brush (middle) works well. A tapered sash brush (bottom) helps with corners on window sash. Use brushes made of hog or ox bristles only with alkyd (oil-based) paints. All-purpose brushes, suitable for all paints, are made with a blend of polyester, nylon, and sometimes animal bristles.

Tips for Choosing Paint Rollers

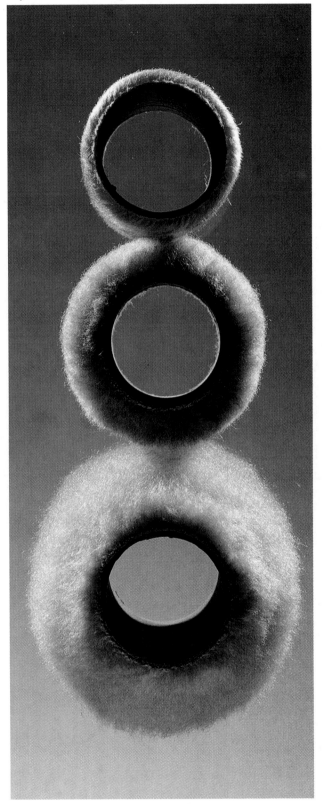

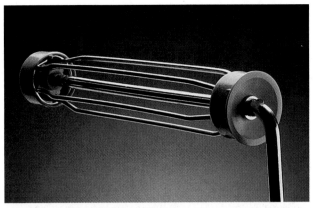

Choose a sturdy 9" roller with a wire cage construction and nylon bearings that roll smoothly. The roller should feel well balanced and have a handle with a threaded end for attaching an extension pole.

Synthetic roller covers (left) are suitable for most paints, especially latexes. For a smoother finish with alkyd paints, use more-expensive lamb's wool or mohair roller covers (right). Mohairs work best with gloss alkyd paints. Better quality roller covers are less likely to shed lint.

Select the proper roller cover for the surface you intend to paint. A ¼"-nap cover (top) is used for very flat surfaces. A ⅜"-nap cover (middle) will hide small flaws found in most flat walls and ceilings. A 1"-nap cover (bottom) fills spaces in rough surfaces, such as concrete blocks, stucco, or heavily textured walls.

Texture rollers apply paint with a consistent, textured surface. They are available in a variety of light and heavy textures and can be used with standard paint or texture paint (see pages 66 to 69). Other specialty rollers and painting pads are available for creating textures and painting unusual surfaces.

How to Use a Paint Roller

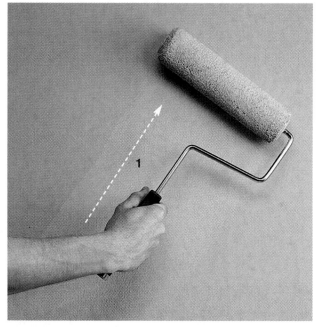

1 Wet the roller cover with water (for latex paint) or mineral spirits (for alkyd enamel), to remove lint and prime the cover. Squeeze out excess liquid. Dip the roller fully into the paint pan reservoir and roll it over the textured ramp to distribute the paint evenly. The roller should be full, but not dripping. Make an upward diagonal sweep about 4 ft. long on the surface, using a slow stroke to avoid splattering.

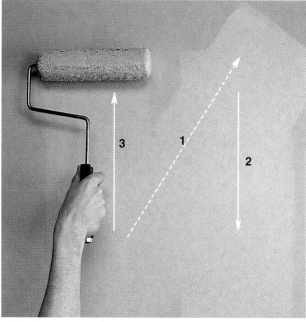

2 Draw the roller straight down (2) from the top of the diagonal sweep made in step 1. Lift and move the roller to the beginning of the diagonal sweep and roll up (3) to complete the unloading of the roller.

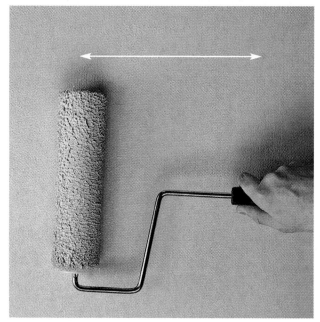

3 Distribute the paint over the rest of the section with horizontal back-and-forth strokes.

4 Smooth the area by lightly drawing the roller vertically from the top to the bottom of the painted area. Lift the roller and return it to the top of the area after each stroke.

How to Use a Paintbrush

1 Dip the brush into the paint, loading one-third of its bristle length. Tap the bristles against the side of the can to remove excess paint, but do not drag the bristles against the lip of the can.

2 Paint along the edges (called "cutting in") using the narrow edge of the brush, pressing just enough to flex the bristles. Keep an eye on the paint edge, and paint with long, slow strokes. Always paint from a dry area back into wet paint to avoid lap marks.

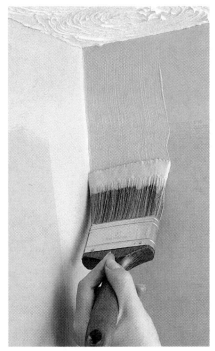

3 Brush wall corners using the wide edge of the brush. Paint open areas with a brush or roller before the brushed paint dries.

4 To paint large areas with a brush, apply the paint with 2 or 3 diagonal strokes. Hold the brush at a 45° angle to the work surface, pressing just enough to flex the bristles. Distribute the paint evenly with horizontal strokes.

5 Smooth the surface by drawing the brush vertically from the top to the bottom of the painted area. Use light strokes and lift the brush from the surface at the end of each stroke. This method is best for slow-drying alkyd enamels.

Painting Walls & Ceilings

For a smooth finish on large wall and ceiling areas, paint in small sections. First use a paintbrush to cut in the edges, then immediately roll the section before moving on. If brushed edges are left to dry before the large surfaces are rolled, visible lap marks will be left on the finished wall. Working in natural light makes it easier to see missed areas.

Spread the paint evenly onto the work surface without letting it run, drip, or lap onto other areas. Excess paint will run on the surface and can drip onto woodwork and floors. Conversely, stretching paint too far leaves lap marks and results in patchy coverage.

For large jobs, mix paint together (called "boxing") in a large pail to eliminate slight color variations between cans. Stir the paint thoroughly with a wooden stick or power drill attachment.

Tips for Painting Walls & Ceilings

Paint to a wet edge. Cut in the edge on small sections with a paintbrush, then immediately roll that section while the edge is still wet. With two painters, let one cut in with a brush while the other rolls the large areas.

Minimize brush marks by sliding the roller cover slightly off of the roller cage when working near wall corners or a ceiling line. Brushed areas dry to a different finish than rolled paint.

How to Paint Ceilings

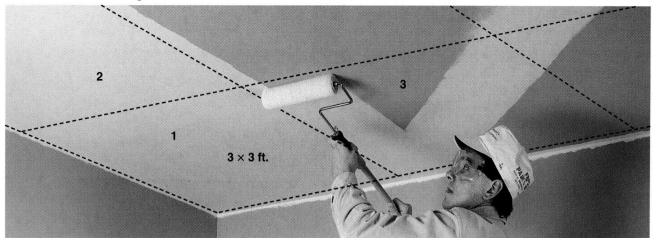

Paint ceilings using a roller handle extension. Use eye protection while painting overhead. Start at the corner farthest from the entry door. Paint the ceiling along the narrow end in 3 × 3-ft. sections, cutting in the edges with a brush before rolling. Apply the paint with a diagonal stroke, then distribute the paint evenly with back-and-forth strokes. For the final smoothing strokes, roll each section toward the wall containing the entry door, lifting the roller at the end of each sweep.

How to Paint Walls

Paint walls in 2 × 4-ft. sections. Start in an upper corner, cutting in the ceiling and wall corners with a brush, then rolling the section. Make the initial diagonal roller stroke from the bottom of the section upward, to avoid dripping paint. Distribute the paint evenly with horizontal strokes, then finish with downward sweeps of the roller. Next, cut in and roll the section directly underneath. Continue with adjacent areas, cutting in and rolling the top sections before the bottom sections. Roll all finish strokes toward the floor.

Decorative Painting

For walls and ceilings that call for more than a monochromatic paint treatment, there's a variety of painting techniques you can use to decorate with self-expression and creativity. Most decorative painting techniques involve a blending of paint colors—to add texture, create an illusion of depth, or to mute, blend, or soften the look of standard paint colors. Four of the most popular painting techniques are shown here: blending, color washing, combing, and stenciling.

The basic tools and materials for decorative painting are simple, but there's a great variety to choose from. For most projects, use latex and acrylic paints. Because they're water-based, latex paints are easy to clean up with just soap and water, and they're also safer for the environment than alkyd (oil-based) paints.

However, because water-based paints dry quickly, they often need an additive to increase the open time, or the length of time the paint can be manipulated. Additives include latex paint conditioners, such as Floetrol, and acrylic paint extenders.

Some decorative techniques call for a paint glaze instead of straight paint. By definition, glaze is a store-bought medium (tinted or untinted) that is similar to paint and can be applied by itself or added to paint to increase its workability and open time. A glaze may also be any mixture combining paint and other mediums to produce a desired color or consistency. The projects shown here that require homemade glazes include a list of ingredients. Paint additives, glazes, and specialty tools are available at paint retailers and craft supply stores.

Acrylic paints are available in a wide range of colors. They can be used alone for stenciling, or mixed with acrylic mediums to create glazes for decorative paint finishes.

Acrylic mediums, or glaze mediums, can be mixed with acrylic or latex paint to create paint glazes with gloss, satin, or matte finishes.

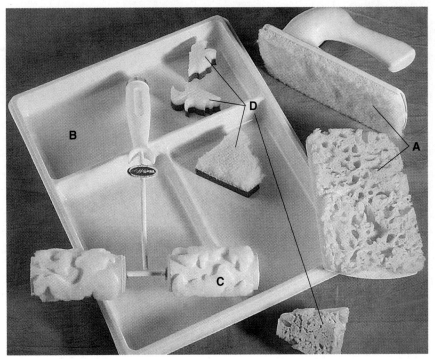

A base coat of paint is required for many decorative finishes. If necessary, prime the surface before painting. Apply the base coat with a roller and brush, following the basic painting techniques shown on pages 72 to 79.

Easy-to-use decorative painting tools are available in kits, which you can add to by purchasing individual accessories. A basic kit may include a handle applicator with interchangeable wool and sea sponge pads (A); a 3-compartment paint tray, for separating paints of different colors (B); a dual-roller with accented roller covers, for creating a blended two-tone finish or a border (C); and edging and finishing tools, to complete designs in corners and small spaces (D).

Blended Finishes

Painting with a blended finish is one of the easiest ways to add new life to a bland room. Using a wool pad or a dual paint roller, you can blend two or more paint colors to create looks from a deeply contrasting texture to a subtle color wash effect. For a bolder pattern, apply related shades that are next to each other on the color wheel, such as orange and yellow.

Consider the colors in your furnishings and floor covering when choosing the paint colors. Select a combination that will harmonize with the room's existing color scheme. The easiest way to select colors is by using a monochromatic paint strip from a paint retailer. Find a strip that works with your color scheme and select paint colors that are at least 2 shades apart on the paint strip.

For a subtle design, choose colors that are 2 to 3 shades apart; for a more textured appearance, select colors that are 4 to 6 shades apart. Or, choose a single color and a neutral shade, such as ivory or white, to create a soft, muted design. The colors shown in this project—deep brown, dark clay, and apricot—blend into a terra cotta finish.

How to Apply a Blended Finish with a Wool Pad

1 Pour each shade of paint into a separate section of a divided paint tray. Add ¼ cup of paint glaze to each color, blending it into the paint with a stir stick. Season the wool pad by wetting your hand with water and running it over the wool to remove lint and loose fibers. Dip the wool pad into the first paint color, and scrape the pad along the edge of the tray to remove excess paint.

Everything You Need

Tools: Divided paint tray, paint stir sticks, wool paint pad, wool edging tool.

Materials: Latex paints, paint glaze.

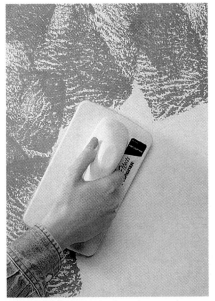

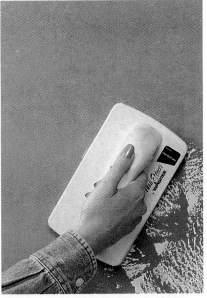

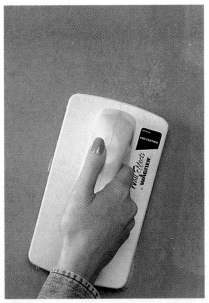

2 Working in a 4 × 4-ft. section, press the pad onto the surface in a random pattern. Cover about 80% of the surface in the section, leaving some bare spots. Scrape the pad on the paint tray to remove as much of the first paint as possible; don't wash the pad before applying the next color.

3 Dip the pad into the second paint color, and remove the excess. Using the same random stamping technique, fill in the bare spots in the section with the second color. When you are finished, scrape the paint from the pad, as before.

4 Dip the wool pad into the third color, and remove the excess. Using the random stamping technique, lightly press the pad onto the painted section. You will begin to see the paint blend. The more you apply the third color, the more the paints will blend and the lighter the final design will be.

5 Once you've finished the section, use a wool edging tool to paint the design into any corners and along the edges of the section. Season the wool tool, as with the pad, then repeat steps 1 through 4, blending the paints until the design is complete. Repeat the process to complete the remaining sections.

Variation: Two-tone Roller. Pour each color of undiluted paint into a section of the paint tray (inset). Coat the rollers and apply the paint using short strokes (about 12"), in alternating vertical, horizontal, and diagonal directions (some manufacturers recommend rolling onto newspaper before rolling wall). The blended effect increases with the amount of rolling.

Color Wash Finishes

Color washing is an easy-to-do paint finish that gives walls a translucent, watercolor look. It can add visual texture to flat drywall surfaces or emphasize the texture of plaster or stucco walls. There are two methods of color washing, each with its own glaze mixture and finish appearance.

The sponge method of color washing calls for a highly diluted glaze that is applied with a natural sea sponge over a base coat of low-luster (eggshell) latex enamel. The result is a subtle texture with a soft blending of colors. The other method—using a brush—involves a heavier glaze that holds more color than the sponge glaze. This finish retains the fine lines of the brush strokes to create a more dramatic effect. As the glaze begins to dry, it can be softened by brushing with a dry, natural-bristle paintbrush.

The color wash glaze can be either lighter or darker than the base coat. For best results, use two colors that are closely related, or consider using a neutral color, like beige or white, for either the base coat or the glaze. Because the glaze is messy to work with, cover the floor and furniture with waterproof drop cloths, and apply painter's tape along the ceiling and moldings.

Color Wash Variations

You can select colors for the base coat and the glaze that are closely related, or use at least one neutral color. A darker glaze over a lighter base coat gives a mottled effect. A lighter glaze over a darker base coat gives a chalky or watercolor effect. The finish above, right, shows a medium turquoise top coat applied over a lighter base coat of white; above, left, is a coral base coat covered with a white top coat.

Color Wash Glazes

Sponge Color Wash:
  1 part latex or acrylic paint
  8 parts water

Brush Color Wash:
  1 part flat latex paint
  1 part latex paint conditioner
  2 parts water

Everything You Need

Tools: Paint roller, pail, natural sea sponge or two 3" to 4" natural-bristle paintbrushes, rubber gloves.

Materials: Low-luster latex enamel paint (for base coat), glaze materials (see above).

How to Color Wash with a Sponge

 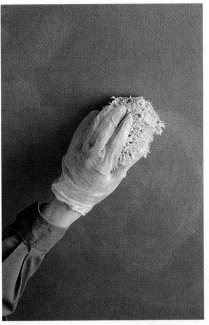 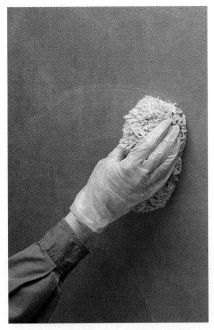

1 Apply a base coat of low-luster latex enamel paint over the entire area, using a paint roller. Allow the paint to dry. Immerse a sea sponge into the color wash glaze. Squeeze out excess liquid, but leave the sponge very wet.

2 Beginning in a low corner, wipe the glaze onto the wall in short, curving strokes. Overlap and change the direction of the strokes, quickly covering a 3 × 3-ft. section of wall.

3 Repeat steps 1 and 2, moving upward and outward until the entire wall has been color washed. Allow the paint to dry. If additional color is desired, apply a second coat.

How to Color Wash with a Brush

1 Apply a base coat of low-luster latex enamel, using a paint roller. Allow the paint to dry. Dip a paintbrush into the color wash glaze, and remove excess glaze by scraping the brush against the pail's rim. Apply the glaze to the wall with cross-hatching strokes, starting from a corner. The more you brush, the softer the appearance will be.

2 If a softer look is desired, brush over the surface, using a dry natural-bristle paintbrush. Wipe excess glaze from the brush as necessary.

Strié & Combed Finishes

Strié and combed finishes are created by similar techniques of dragging a tool over wet glaze to reveal a base coat of a different color. The result is a textured, linear pattern, which can run in vertical lines, curves, swirls, zig-zags, or a weave pattern resembling fabric. Both finishes start with a base coat of low-luster (eggshell) latex enamel, followed by a latex or acrylic glaze mixture.

The strié effect is created using a dry, natural-bristle brush, resulting in fine, irregular streaks and an interesting blend of color variations. A combed finish can be made with a variety of specialty tools, offering a range of patterns and designs. An additional option for the combed finish is to use a thickened glaze, giving a more opaque look with distinct lines and texture.

Since the glaze must be wet for brushing or combing, timing is important. It's helpful to have an assistant for large surfaces. After one person has applied the glaze, the other brushes or combs through the glaze before it dries. If you're working alone, work in smaller sections. It's a good idea to practice the technique on mat board and experiment with different glaze thicknesses before painting the wall.

How to Apply a Strié Finish

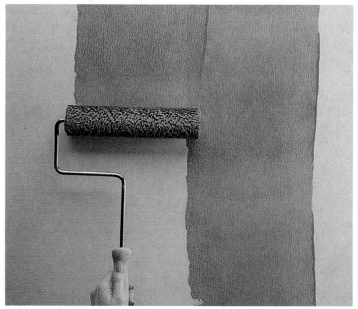

1 Apply the base coat of low-luster latex enamel, and allow the paint to dry. Mix the glaze (see chart, left). Apply the glaze over the base coat in a vertical section about 18" wide, using a paint roller or natural-bristle paintbrush.

Glazes for Strié & Combed Finishes

Basic Glaze:

    1 part latex or craft acrylic paint
    1 part latex paint conditioner
    1 part water

Thickened Glaze:

    2 parts latex or craft acrylic paint
    1 part acrylic paint thickener (may be used with latex paints)

Everything You Need

Tools: Paint roller or natural-bristle paintbrush, wide natural-bristle brush, soft natural-bristle paintbrush, combing tool (optional).

Materials: Low-luster latex enamel paint (for base coat), glaze materials (see above), rags.

Techniques for Applying a Combed Finish

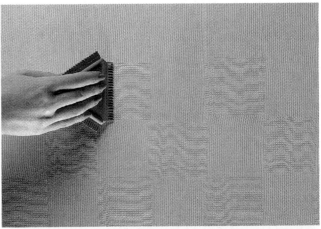

Create a check pattern using a rubber comb (right, top). After each pass, wipe off the tool with a dry rag to ensure clean lines.

A stipple pad makes a variety of designs (right, bottom). For a denim look, drag through the glaze vertically, then horizontally.

Use a rubber squeegee for swirls, scallops, and wavy lines (below). Wipe off excess glaze frequently.

2 Drag a dry, wide, natural-bristle brush through the glaze just after it's applied. Work from top to bottom in continuous strokes, holding the bristles rigid with the handle tilted toward you. Repeat until the desired effect is achieved.

3 Wipe the brush occasionally on a clean, dry rag to remove excess glaze and ensure a uniform strié look. Or, rinse the brush in clear water, and wipe it dry.

4 For softer lines, brush the surface lightly after the glaze has dried for about 5 minutes. Use a soft natural-bristle brush, making the brush stokes in the same direction as the streaks.

Stenciled Designs

Use stenciled motifs to highlight areas or create decorative borders. A variety of precut stencils is available in a wide range of prices, typically determined by the intricacy of the design, or you can make custom stencils by tracing designs onto transparent Mylar sheets. For stencils that coordinate with home furnishings, adapt a design from wallpaper, fabric, or artwork. Use a photocopier to enlarge or reduce patterns to the desired size.

Most precut stencils have a separate plate for each color and are numbered according to the sequence of use. You can use a single stencil plate for multiple colors if the spaces between the design areas are large enough to be covered with masking tape. When stenciling multicolored designs, apply the largest part of the design first. When stenciling borders, it's usually best to apply all the repeats of the first color before applying the second color.

Before starting your project, carefully plan the placement of the design. Stencil the design onto paper, and tape it to the surface to check for placement. Border designs with obvious repeats, such as swags or bows, require careful planning to avoid partial motifs. If you are stenciling a border, the placement may be influenced by the position of room details, such as windows, doors, and heating vents. It's usually best to start at the most prominent area and work outward. If necessary, you can adjust the spacing between border repeats.

Use high-quality, stiff stencil brushes in sizes appropriate for the space being stenciled. Clean the brush and allow it to dry before reusing it, or use a separate brush for each color. You can stencil over any clean, painted surface. If the surface is finished wood, apply a clear finish or sealer to the entire surface after stenciling.

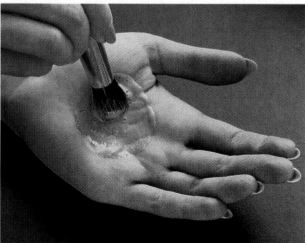

Tip: Clean acrylic paint from stencil brushes by applying a small amount of dishwashing detergent to the brush. Rub the bristles in the palm of your hand in a circular motion until all of the paint is removed. Rinse with water and allow the bristles to dry. To remove oil-based paint, first clean the brush with mineral spirits and dry it on paper towels. Then, wash the brush with detergent and rinse with water.

Everything You Need

Tools: Level, stencil brushes, artist's brush.

Materials: Pre-cut or custom stencil, masking tape, spray adhesive (optional), craft acrylic paints or liquid or solid oil-based stencil paints, disposable plates, paper towels.

For custom stencils: Paper, colored pencils, transparent Mylar sheets, masking tape, fine-point permanent marker, self-healing cutting board or cardboard, mat knife, metal ruler.

How to Make a Custom Stencil

1 Draw or trace the design onto a sheet of paper. Repeat the design, if necessary, so it is 13" to 18" long, making sure the spacing between repeats is consistent. Color the design, using colored pencils. Mark placement lines to help you position the stencil on the wall.

2 Position a Mylar sheet over the design so the edges of the sheet extend beyond the top and bottom of the design by at least 1". Secure the sheet with masking tape. Trace the areas that will be stenciled in the first color, using a marker. Transfer the placement lines.

3 Trace the design areas for each additional color onto a separate Mylar sheet. To help you align the stencil, outline the areas for previous colors with dotted lines. Layer all of the Mylar sheets, and check for accuracy. Using a mat knife and straightedge, trim the outer edges of the stencil plates, leaving a 1" to 3" border around the design.

4 Separate the Mylar sheets. Cut out the traced areas on each sheet, using a mat knife. Cut the smallest shapes first, then the larger ones. Pull the knife toward you as you cut, turning the Mylar sheet, rather than the knife, to change the cutting direction.

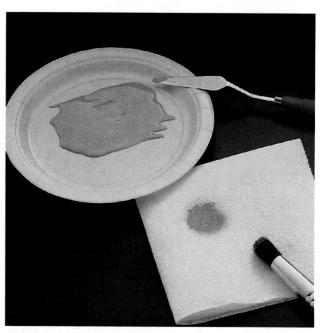

1 Mark the placement for the stencil on the surface with masking tape. Or, draw a light reference line, using a level and a pencil. Position the stencil plate for the first color, aligning the placement line with the tape or pencil line. Secure the stencil in place with masking tape or spray adhesive.

2 Pour 1 to 2 teaspoons of acrylic or oil-based paint onto a disposable plate. Dip the tip of a stencil brush into the paint. Blot the brush onto a folded paper towel, using a circular motion, until the bristles are almost dry.

Variation: To stencil with solid paint, or *crayon* paint, remove the protective coating from the crayon tip, using a paper towel. Rub a 1½" circle of paint onto a blank area of the stencil. Load a stencil brush by lightly rubbing the brush over the paint in a circular motion, first in one direction, then in the other.

3 Hold the brush perpendicular to the surface. Apply the paint within the cut areas of the stencil, using a circular motion. Stencil all of the cut areas of the first stencil plate, and allow the paint to dry. Remove the stencil.

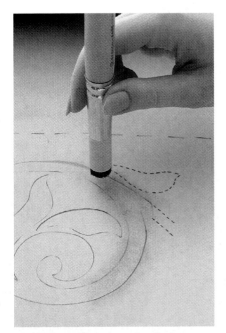

4 Secure the second plate to the surface, matching the design. Apply the second paint color in the appropriate areas. Repeat the process for remaining stencils and colors until the design is complete.

5 After all of the paints are completely dry, touch up any glitches or smudges on the surface, using background paint and an artist's brush.

Variation: Use the stippling method for a deeper, textured appearance: Wrap masking tape around the bristles of a stenciling brush, ¼" from the ends. Hold the brush perpendicular to the surface, and apply the paint with a dabbing motion.

Tips for Stenciling Shaded Designs

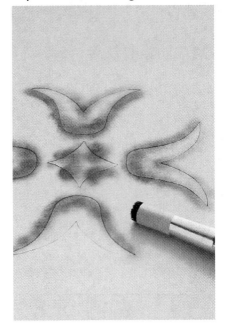

Apply paint within the cut areas of the stencil, leaving the centers lighter than the edges. For an aged, fade-away effect, use a heavier touch at the base of the motif and a lighter touch at the top.

Add a complementary color or darker color of paint for additional shading along the outer edges of the cut areas.

Hold a piece of Mylar in place to cover a painted portion of the area, and apply paint next to the edge of the Mylar. For example, cover one-half of a leaf to stencil the veins.

Wallcovering

Vinyl

Foils

Grasscloth

Fabric

Embossed

Very few modern "wallpapers" are actually made of paper. Today's wallcoverings may be made of vinyl, vinyl-coated paper or cloth, textiles, natural grasses, foil, or Mylar. Vinyl or coated vinyl coverings are the easiest to hang, clean, and remove. Other types of wallcoverings offer specific decorative effects but may require special handling.

Tools for hanging wallcovering include ordinary items and a few specialty tools. Use a bubble-stick or 4-ft. level and a pencil to mark layout lines. Never mark with ink pens or chalk lines, which can bleed through the wet wallcovering or ooze from the seams. Cut wallcovering with a sharp utility knife and a straightedge. Use non-corrosive paint pails to hold wash water, and a natural or high-quality plastic sponge to wash wallcovering.

To smooth the wallcovering as you apply it, use a smoothing brush. Brushes come in various nap lengths. Use a short-nap brush for vinyl wallcoverings and a soft, long-nap brush for fragile materials, such as grasscloths. A seam roller makes it easy to smooth the joints between strips. Pages 94 to 95 show you the basic wallcovering tools and handling techniques.

If your wallcovering is not prepasted, you'll need one or more types of adhesive. For most vinyl or vinyl-backed wallcoverings, choose a heavy-duty premixed vinyl adhesive that contains a mildew inhibitor. Vinyl wallcoverings also require a special vinyl-on-vinyl adhesive for areas where the wallcovering strips overlap or for installing vinyl borders over wallcovering. Specialty wallcoverings may need special adhesives; check the label or ask a dealer about the correct adhesive for your application. You can apply adhesives with an ordinary paint roller.

Before hanging wallcovering, make sure the wall surfaces are both sealed and sized to prevent the adhesives from soaking into the surface. Today's premixed primer-sealers do both jobs with a single application.

Tips for Choosing Wallcovering

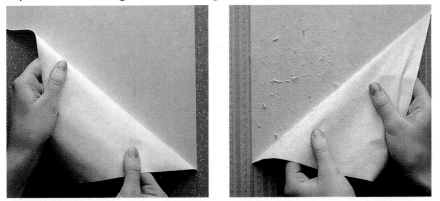

Removability: Strippable wallcoverings (left) can be pulled away from the wall by hand, leaving little or no film or residue. Peelable wallcoverings (right) can be removed but may leave a thin paper layer on the wall, which can usually be removed with soap and water. Check the back of the sample or the wallcovering package for its strippability rating. Choose a strippable product to make future redecorating easier.

Cleaning: *Washable* wallcoverings can be cleaned with mild soap and water and a sponge. *Scrubbable* wallcoverings are durable enough to be scrubbed with a soft brush. Choose a scrubbable type for heavy-use areas.

Application: Prepasted wallcoverings (left) are factory-coated with water-based adhesive that is activated when the wallcovering is wetted in a water tray. Unpasted wallcoverings (right) must be coated with an adhesive for hanging. Prepasted products are easier to prepare and just as durable as those requiring an adhesive coat.

Dye-lot: To avoid slight color differences, make sure all of the wallcovering you use comes from the same dye lot. Also, record dye-lot numbers for future reference.

Packaging: Wallcoverings are sold in continuous triple-, double-, and single-roll bolts.

Patterns: There is always more waste with large patterns. A wallcovering with a large drop pattern can be more expensive to hang than one with a smaller repeat. With large designs, it may also be difficult to avoid pattern interruptions at baseboards or corners.

How to Handle Prepasted Wallcovering

1 Fill a water tray half full of lukewarm water. Roll the cut strip loosely with the pattern side in. Soak the roll in the tray as directed by the manufacturer, usually about 1 minute. Pulling from one end, lift the strip from the water, making sure the back side is evenly wetted.

2 "Book" the strip by folding both ends into the center, with the pasted side in. Do not crease the folds. Let the strip cure for about 10 minutes. Some wallcoverings should not be booked; follow the manufacturer's directions. For ceiling strips or wallcovering borders, use an "accordion" book (inset).

How to Position & Smooth Wallcovering

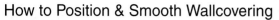

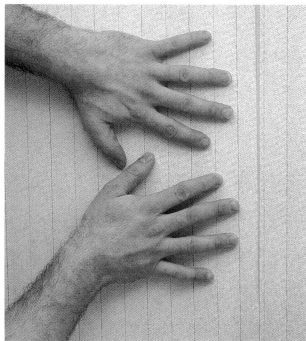

1 Unfold the booked strip and position it lightly with its edge butted against a plumb line or previous strip. Use flat palms to slide the strip precisely into place. Flatten the top of the strip with a smoothing brush.

2 Beginning at the top, smooth the wallcovering out from the center in both directions. Check for bubbles, and make sure the seams are properly butted. If necessary, pull the strip away and reposition it.

How to Trim Wallcovering

1 Position a 10" or 12" drywall knife along the cut, then cut along the edge with a sharp utility knife. Keep the utility knife blade in place while changing the position of the drywall knife.

2 With wallcovered ceilings, crease the wall strips with the drywall knife, then cut along the crease with scissors. Cutting with a utility knife may puncture the ceiling strip.

How to Roll Seams

Let the strips stand for about ½ hour. Then, roll the seam gently with a seam roller. Do not press out the adhesive by rolling too much or too forcefully. Do not roll seams on foils, fabrics, or embossed wallcoverings. Instead, tap the seams gently with a smoothing brush.

How to Rinse Wallcovering

Use clear water and a sponge to rinse adhesive from the surface. Change the water after every 3 or 4 strips. Do not let water run along the seams. Do not use water on grasscloths, embossed wallcoverings, or fabrics.

Measuring & Estimating for Wallcovering

Calculate the square footage of your walls and ceilings, then refer to the coverage information listed on the wallcovering package to estimate the correct amount of wallcovering to buy. Because of normal trimming waste, the actual per-roll coverage of wallcovering will be at least 15% less than the coverage listed on the package. The waste percentage can be higher depending on how much space it takes for the wallcovering pattern to repeat itself. This "pattern repeat" measurement is listed on the wallcovering package. When estimating, add the pattern repeat measurement to the wall height measurement of the room.

Measure the room:

Walls: Measure the length and height of the walls to the nearest ½ ft. Include window and door openings but not baseboards or crown moldings.

Ceilings: Measure the length and the width of ceiling to the nearest ½ ft.

How to Measure Unusual Surfaces

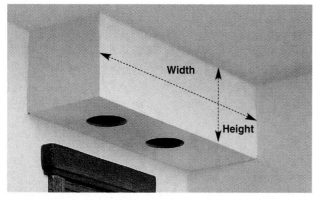

Soffits: If you're covering the sides of a soffit, add the width and height of each side to the wall measurement.

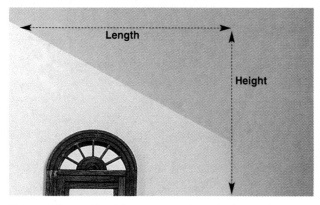

Triangular walls: Measure as though the surface is square: length × height.

How to Figure Actual Per-roll Coverage

1) Total per-roll coverage (square feet)	
2) Adjust for waste factor	× .85
3) Actual per-roll coverage (square feet)	=

How to Calculate Rolls Needed for a Ceiling

1) Room length (feet)	
2) Wallcovering pattern repeat (feet)	+
3) Adjusted length (feet)	=
4) Room width (feet)	×
5) Ceiling area (square feet)	=
6) Actual per-roll coverage (figured above; square feet)	÷
7) Number of rolls needed for ceiling	=

How to Calculate Rolls Needed for Walls

1) Wall height (feet)	
2) Wallcovering pattern repeat (feet)	+
3) Adjusted height (feet)	=
4) Wall length; or room perimeter (feet)	×
5) Wall area (square feet)	=
6) Actual per-roll coverage (figured above; square feet)	÷
7) Number of rolls	=
8) Add 1 roll for each archway or recessed window	+
9) Number of rolls needed for walls	=

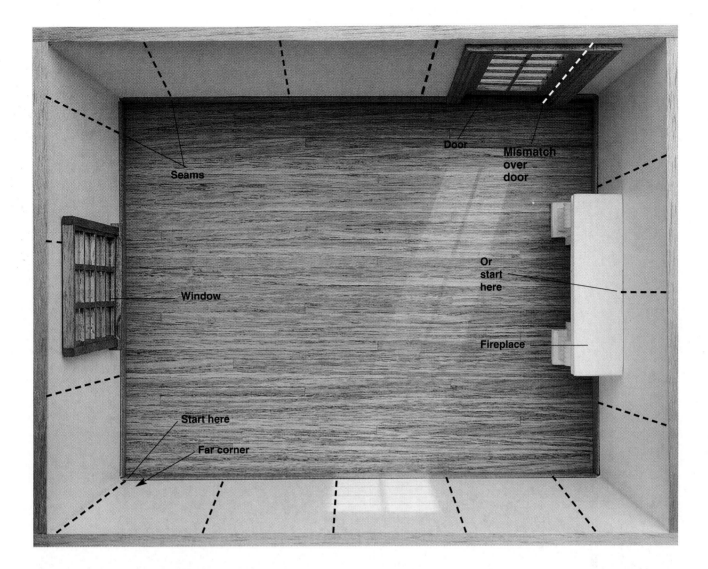

Seams

Door

Mismatch
over
door

Window

Or
start
here

Fireplace

Start here

Far corner

The Hanging Plan

For best results, devise a hanging plan by sketching out the seam locations. When hanging any patterned wallcovering, there will be one seam where a full strip meets a partial strip, usually resulting in a mismatch of the pattern. Plan so that this seam falls in an inconspicuous spot, like behind a door or above an entrance. If one or more seams falls in a bad spot, adjust your plumb line a few inches to compensate. Follow these tips for a successful hanging plan:

• *Plan the mismatch.* If the room has no obvious focal point, start at the corner farthest from the entry. Measure out a distance equal to the wall-covering width and mark a point. Work in both directions, marking each seam location.

• *Start at a focal point,* like a fireplace or large window. Center a plumb line on the focal point, then sketch a plan in both directions from the centerline.

• *Adjust for corners* that fall exactly on seam lines. Make sure you have at least ½" overlap on inside corners, and 1" on outside corners.

• *Adjust for seams* that fall in difficult locations, such as near the edges of windows or doors. Shift your starting point so that the seams leave you with workable widths of wallcovering around these obstacles.

• *Plan a ceiling layout* so that any pattern interruption will fall along the least conspicuous side of the room. Pattern interruptions occur on the last ceiling strip, so start the layout on the side opposite the entry.

Installing Wallcovering

Working with wallcovering is easier with a helper, especially on ceilings. Shut off the electricity to the room at the main service panel, and remove the receptacle and switch coverplates. Cover the outlets with masking tape.

For ceilings, remember that the pattern on the last strip may be broken by the ceiling line. Since the least visible edge is usually on the entry wall, begin hanging strips at the far end of the room, and work toward the entryway. If you're covering the walls as well as the ceiling, remember that the ceiling pattern can blend perfectly into only one wall.

Everything You Need

Tools: Bubblestick or level, pencil, smoothing brush, water tray (for prepasted wallcovering), paint roller and tray (for unpasted wallcovering), scissors, utility knife, drywall knives, sponge, bucket, seam roller.

Materials: Wallcovering, adhesive (for unpasted wallcovering), vinyl-on-vinyl adhesive (for vinyl wallcovering).

How to Apply Wallcovering to Ceilings

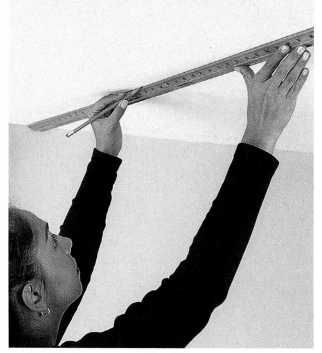

1 Measure the width of the wallcovering strip and subtract ½". Near a corner, measure this distance away from the wall at several points, and mark points on the ceiling with a pencil.

2 Using the marks as guides, draw a guide line along the length of the ceiling with a pencil and straightedge. Cut and prepare the first wallcovering strip (see pages 94 to 95).

3 Working in small sections, position the strip against the guide line. Overlap the side wall by ½", and the end wall by 2". Flatten the strip with a smoothing brush as you work. Trim each strip after it is smoothed.

4 Cut out a small wedge of wallcovering in the corner so that the strip will lie flat. Press the wallcovering into the corner with a drywall knife.

5 If the end walls will also be covered, trim the ceiling overlap to ½". Leave a ½" overlap on all walls that will be covered with matching wallcovering.

Variation: Trim the excess at the corner. Continue hanging strips, butting the edges so that the pattern matches.

How to Apply Wallcovering to Walls

1 Measure from your starting point a distance equal to the wallpaper width minus ½" and mark a point. At that point draw a vertical plumb line from the ceiling to the floor, using a bubblestick or level.

2 Cut the first strip to length with about 2" of excess at each end. Prepare the strip according to the manufacturer's directions. Unfold the top portion of the booked strip and position it against the line so the strip overlaps onto the ceiling about 2".

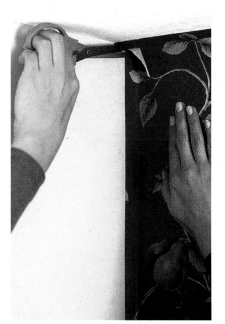

3 Snip the top corner of the strip so the wallcovering wraps around the corner without wrinkling. Slide the strip into position with open palms then smooth it with a smoothing brush.

4 Unfold the bottom of the strip and use flat palms to position the strip against the plumb line. Smooth the strip flat with a smoothing brush, carefully pressing out any bubbles.

5 Trim the excess wallcovering with a drywall knife and a sharp utility knife. Rinse any adhesive from the surface using clear water and a sponge.

6 Hang additional strips, butting the edges so that the pattern matches. Let the strips stand for about ½ hour, then use a seam roller to roll the seams lightly. (On embossed wallcoverings or fabrics, tap the seams gently with a smoothing brush.)

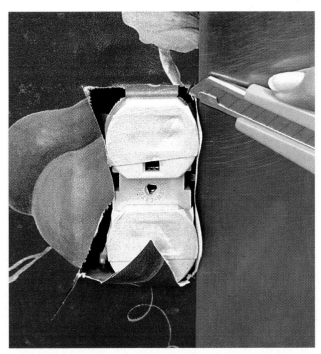

7 With the power off, hang wallcovering over receptacle and switch boxes, then use a drywall knife and utility knife to trim back the paper to the edges of the box.

How to Apply Wallcovering Around Corners

1 Measure from the edge of the preceding strip to the corner at several points, then add ½" to the longest of these measurements. Align the edges of a booked strip, then measure from the edge and mark the above distance at two points. Cut the strip using a straightedge and utility knife.

2 Position the strip on the wall, overlapping slightly onto the uncovered wall. Cut slits at the top and bottom so the strip wraps smoothly. Flatten the strip with a smoothing brush and trim the excess at the top and bottom.

(continued next page)

3 On the uncovered wall, measure from the corner and mark at a distance equal to the width of the leftover strip plus ½". Draw a plumb line from the ceiling to the floor. Using the same measurement, cut a new strip to that width, starting from the leading edge of the new strip, so the pattern will match at the corner.

4 Position the new cut strip on the wall with the cut edge in the corner and the leading (uncut) edge along the plumb line. Press the strip flat and smooth it with a smoothing brush, then trim the excess at the ceiling and baseboard.

5 If you are using vinyl wallcovering, peel back the edge at the corner and apply vinyl-on-vinyl adhesive to the seam. Press the overlapping strip flat and let it stand for ½ hour, then roll the seam and rinse the area with a damp sponge.

Variation: Outside corners usually can be wrapped around without cutting the strip and drawing a new plumb line. If the corner is not plumb, follow the directions for inside corners, except add 1" to the measurement in step 1, rather than ½". If necessary, trim the top wallcovering strip to follow the corner.

How to Apply Wallcovering Around a Window or Door

1 Position the strip on the wall, running over the window or door casing. Butt the seam against the edge of the preceding strip. Smooth the flat areas with a smoothing brush and press the strip tightly against the casing.

2 Use scissors to cut diagonally from the edge of the strip to the corners of the casing. Then trim away the excess wallcovering using a drywall knife and a utility knife. Rinse the wallcovering and casing with a damp sponge.

3 Cut a short strip for the section above the door, or for the sections above and below the window. Hang these strips exactly vertically to ensure a pattern match for the next full strip.

4 Repeat steps 1 and 2 to install the strip along the other side of the casing, matching the edges.

How to Apply Wallcovering Borders

1 If you're applying the border in the middle of a wall, draw a light pencil line around the room at the desired height, using a level. Cut the first border strip. Prepare the strip, following the manufacturer's directions, and book it accordion-style (see page 94).

2 Beginning at the least conspicuous corner, over-lap the border onto the adjacent wall ½". Have a helper hold the border while you apply it and smooth it with a smoothing brush.

3 At the inside corner, create a ¼" tuck from the overlap. Apply the adjoining border strip, trimming it flush with the corner, using a utility knife.

4 Peel back the tucked strip, and smooth the strip around the corner, overlapping the border on the adjacent wall. Press the border flat. Apply seam adhesive to the lapped seam, if necessary.

5 Where seams fall in the middle of a wall, overlap the border strips so the patterns match. Cut through both layers, using a utility knife and a drywall knife. Peel back the borders and remove the cut ends. Press the strips flat. Roll the seam after ½ hour, and rinse with a damp sponge.

6 Trim the border at door and window casings by holding the border against the outer edge of the casing with a drywall knife and trimming the excess with a utility knife. Rinse the border and casing with a damp sponge.

How to Miter Border Corners

1 Apply the horizontal border strips, extending them past the corners a distance greater than the width of the border. Apply the vertical border strips, overlapping the horizontal strips.

2 Hold a straightedge along the points where the border strips intersect, and cut through both layers, using a utility knife. Peel back the strips and remove the cut ends.

3 Press the border back in place. Lightly roll the seam after ½ hour. Rinse any adhesive from the border, using a damp sponge.

Crown molding

Picture rail

Casing

Chair rail

Baseboard

Base shoe

Installing Trim

The term *trim* refers to all of the moldings that dress up walls and ceilings, hide gaps and joints between surfaces, and adorn window and door frames. As a decorating tool, trim lends a sculptural quality to otherwise flat surfaces and can have a dramatic effect on any room in the house. Working with trim involves a few specific cuts and techniques, but once you learn them, you can install almost any type.

The photo at left shows many of the standard types of trim molding:

Crown molding (page 112) decorates the inter-sections of walls and ceilings. Most crown mold-ing is sprung, meaning it installs at an angle to its nailing surfaces, leaving a hollow space be-hind it. Crown molding can be installed by itself or as part of a more elaborate, built-up molding treatment, called a cornice (page 113). In addi-tion to wood, crown molding can be made with plastic polymers, often in ornate, one-piece styles (pages 116 to 117).

Picture rail is a traditional molding with a novel function: it has a protruding, rounded edge that holds hooks for hanging pictures with wire. It can stand alone on a wall or be installed so that it adds contour to a crown or cornice molding (see page 115).

Casing (pages 118 to 119) is trim that covers the edges of door and window frames.

Chair rail runs horizontally along walls at a height of 30" to 36", typically. It originated as a way to protect walls from collisions with chair backs, but today, it's more often used to divide a wall visually, serving as a border for a wallpaper wainscot or a transition between different paint colors.

NOTE: Install chair rail and picture rail as you would baseboard.

Baseboard (page 111) covers the bottoms of walls along the floor. Styles range from single-piece to built-up versions that include a base cap and a base shoe installed at the floor. Base shoe is small, typically rounded molding that is flexible and can follow contours in the floor to hide gaps left by the baseboard.

Wall frame molding (pages 120 to 121), not shown at left, is a decorative wall treatment made from four molding pieces installed to cre-ate the effect of a picture frame.

Tips for Cutting Trim

A basic miter box, made of wood or metal, and a backsaw are the simplest tools for making clean cuts in trim. These typically cut only 45° and 90° angles. A backsaw is a short handsaw with a stiff spine that keeps the blade straight while cutting.

Swivel-type miter boxes rotate and lock the saw into position for cutting a wide range of angles. Some types have a special saw affixed to the miter box; others have clamps that accept standard backsaws.

Power miter saws make very clean, accurate cuts and are the best tools for cutting trim. The saw swivels on its base and locks into position. Standard miter saws are fixed vertically, while compound miter saws tilt to make bevel and miter cuts in one stroke.

Tips for Fastening Trim

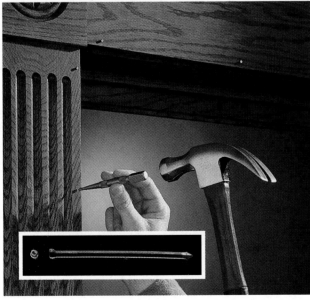

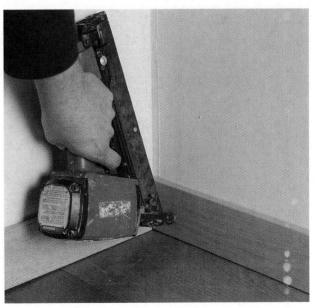

Finish nails are the best fasteners for most trim (inset). Drive the nails close to the surface with a hammer, then countersink, or set, them about 1/16" deep into the wood, using a nail set with a point slightly smaller than the nail head. Drill pilot holes for the nails in hardwood or small pieces of trim, to prevent splitting. As a minimum, nails should be long enough to penetrate the supporting material by 3/4"; heavier moldings require longer nails.

Pneumatic nailers automatically drive special finish nails using compressed air. Air nailers simplify your work considerably by allowing you to hold the trim while nailing and eliminating the banging caused by hammering. They eliminate the need for pilot holes and countersink the nails automatically. Rental centers carry nail guns, air compressors, and nails in various sizes.

Standard Trim Joints

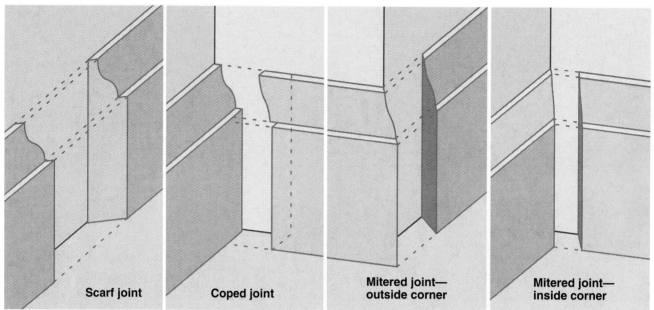

Scarf joint

Coped joint

Mitered joint— outside corner

Mitered joint— inside corner

The basic joints for installing most trim are shown here. A scarf joint joins two pieces along a length of wall. Coped joints join contoured molding at inside corners: the first piece is butted into the corner; the second piece is cut and fitted against the face of the first. Coped joints are less likely than mitered joints to show gaps if the wood shrinks. Mitered joints are used at outside and inside corners. They're typically made with two pieces cut at a 45° angle, but the angle may vary depending on the shape of the corner. Uncontoured moldings can also be butted together at inside corners (see page 111).

How to Make Mitered Joints

A mitered joint is made with two pieces cut at the same angle. Cut the pieces on a miter saw for accuracy. If the corner is not 90°, cut each piece at ½ the total angle of the corner (example: if the corner is 45°, cut the pieces at 22½°).

A handy technique for measuring and fitting mitered joints is to make a pattern piece with opposing miter cuts at the ends. Hold the pattern against the wall at corners to test-fit and position your workpieces. Cut a pattern for both inside and outside corners.

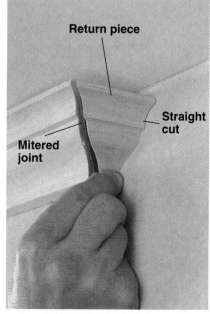

Return piece

Straight cut

Mitered joint

Mitered returns finish molding ends that would otherwise be exposed. Miter the main piece as you would at an outside corner. Cut a miter on the return piece, then cut it to length with a straight cut so it butts to the wall. Attach the return piece with wood glue.

How to Make Coped Joints

1 A coped joint is the best inside corner joint for contoured molding. Install the first molding piece with its end butted tight to the corner. Cut the second piece at a 45° angle so that the grain is exposed on the front side.

2 Using a coping saw, cut along the front edge of the molding, following the contour exactly. Angle the saw toward the back side of the molding at 30° to 45° to create a sharp edge along the contour. If the bottom edge of the molding will be visible, such as with crown molding, you may need to make a straight cut at that edge before starting the contoured cut. Test-fit the coped cut against the installed piece. If necessary, make adjustments, using sandpaper, a file, or a utility knife.

How to Make Scarf Joints

Scarf joints (or *field* joints) are used for joining molding on long runs. They help hide gaps if the wood shrinks. To make a scarf joint, cut the first piece at 45° so the end grain shows at the front. Install the piece, but don't nail it within 2 ft. of the joint. Cut the second piece at 45° in the opposite direction from the first. Fit the joint together, then fasten both pieces.

For crown and other sprung molding, cut the first piece at a 30° angle. Install the first piece, but nail only to within 2 ft. of the joint. Cut the second piece at 30° in the opposite direction—it's best if you can do this without adjusting the saw between cuts. Test-fit the joint, then apply wood glue to the mating surfaces and fasten both pieces completely.

How to Plan Your Trim Layout

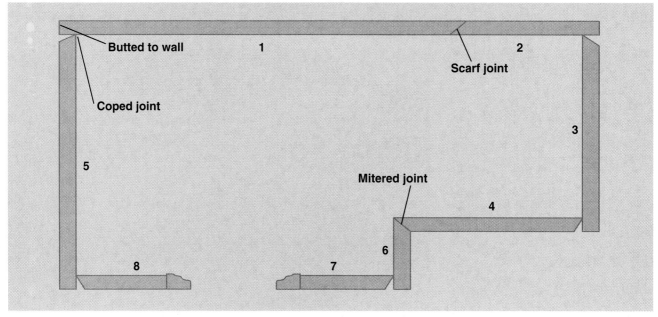

Plan the order of your trim installation to minimize the number of difficult cuts on individual pieces. Use the longest pieces of molding for the most visible walls, saving the shorter ones for less conspicuous areas. When possible, place the joints so they point away from the direct line of sight from the room's entrance. If a piece will be coped on one end and mitered on the other, such as #4 above, cut and fit the coped end first. Also keep in mind the nailing points—mark all framing members you'll be nailing into before starting the installation (see below). As a minimum, all trim should be nailed at every wall stud, and every ceiling joist, if applicable. Install door and window casing before installing horizontal molding that will butt into it.

Tips for Locating & Marking Studs & Joists

Use a studfinder, an electronic device that uses sonic waves to locate framing behind the wall or ceiling surface. Studfinders locate the edges of framing so you can determine the center of studs and joists.

Look along trim for nails, which indicate framing locations. Wall receptacles typically are installed on studs. Visible drywall seams and popped fasteners also indicate studs and joists.

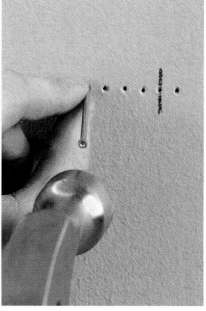

Confirm framing locations by driving a finish nail through the wall surface. Nail every ¼" until you find both edges of the framing member. Mark the edges and center. Measure from the centerpoint to find neighboring members—typically 16" or 24" apart.

How to Install Baseboard

Start by locating and marking the wall studs. Cut the ends of the first piece to fit from corner to corner. If you're using a butted or coped joint at the inside corners, cut the piece long by about 1/16", then bend it out at the center and spring it into place against the wall. If you're mitering the inside corners, test-fit the piece using a pattern (see page 108). Nail the first piece as shown in the illustration below (right). Butt the second piece tightly against the face of the first piece and fasten it.

Variation: If you have contoured molding and you're coping the inside corners, cope the second piece to follow the profile of the first (see page 109). If the other end of the second piece is butted into a corner, cut the piece long by 1/16", and spring it into place.

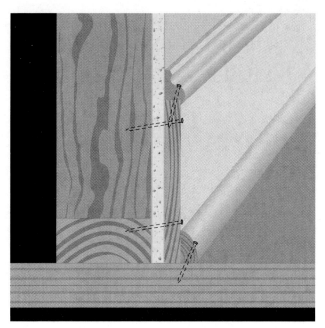

Mark molding at outside corners by fitting the end of the piece into the corner (butting, mitering, or coping it, according to your plan), then marking where the back side of the molding meets the outside corner of the wall. Cut the outside end at 45°, and test-fit the piece using a pattern. Fasten the piece, stopping about 2 ft. short of the outside corner. Complete the nailing when the mating piece is in place.

Fasten the baseboard as shown here, nailing the main baseboard into the wall studs and bottom plate at each stud location. If you're installing a built-up molding, run the main baseboard first, then add the cap and base shoe. Nail the cap into the baseboard or the wall studs, depending on the thickness of the baseboard. Nail the shoe to the floor only, to prevent gapping if the baseboard shrinks.

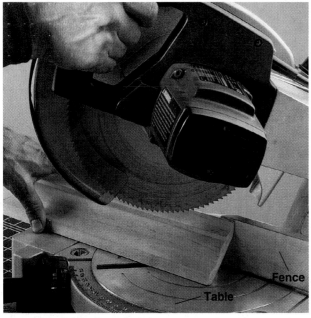

Make angled cuts on crown molding by placing the molding on the miter saw (or miter box) upside down and backward from how it will be installed. Think of the saw fence as the wall and the saw table as the ceiling. Hold the molding tightly in place so the back surfaces are flush to the table and fence. Cut test pieces before cutting any workpieces. To make square cuts, lay the molding flat on the saw table.

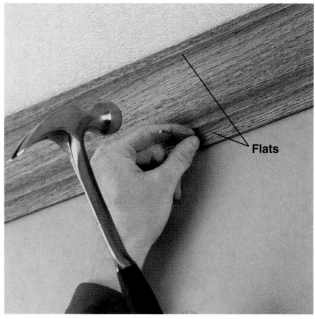

Locate and mark the framing members. Cut molding to fit between two corners. If both ends are at inside corners, cut the piece long by about 1/16", then bend it out in the center and let it spring into place. Fasten the molding with finish nails through the flats of the molding—one at the top edge and one at the lower edge—at each framing location. Offset the nails slightly so they're not aligned vertically.

Variation: Where there's no framing to nail into, such as along walls parallel to joists, secure the top edge of molding with construction adhesive. Using an air nailer, drive pairs of nails at opposing angles every 16" along the top flat. Nail the bottom edge at each stud location.

Use coped joints at inside corners (see page 109). If necessary, use a file or rasp to remove material along the end grain of the piece, being careful not to file the edge of the coped cut. If the piece is coped at both ends, cut it long by about 1/16" and spring it into place.

Miter outside corners, cutting each piece at 45°. Use a pattern with mitered ends to help position your workpieces. Fasten the first piece of each joint to within 2 ft. of the corner, leaving some flexibility for making adjustments when you install the adjoining piece.

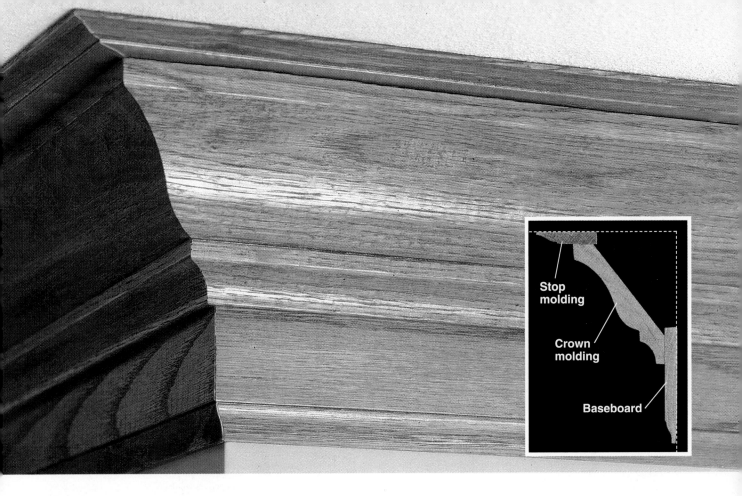

Stop
molding

Crown
molding

Baseboard

Creating a Built-up Cornice

A cornice essentially is an elaborate crown molding, decorating the area where the walls meet the ceiling. Traditionally, cornices have been made with plaster, a solid piece of wood, or a combination of relatively simple molding pieces—called a *built-up* cornice. Built-up types are the most common today because they're much cheaper and easier to install than their counterparts, and they allow for a custom design.

To design your own cornice, visit a well-stocked lumberyard or home center and gather several molding samples of different types: baseboard, stop, crown or sprung cove, as well as some smaller trims, like quarter-rounds and coves. At home, arrange the samples in different combinations and positions to find the best design.

There are a couple of things to keep in mind as you design. The first is moderation. It's easy to overwhelm a room with a cornice that's too big or complicated, so try to keep things in perspective. Also take into account the size of the baseboard, if the room has one. A baseboard creates a visual balance with a cornice, and the two should be roughly proportionate. The second consideration is backing. All of the molding

pieces must be fastened—to wall studs, ceiling joists, pre-installed blocking, or other moldings—so think about where your nails will go. One of the variations on page 115 shows a simple way to build a cornice around 2 × 2 blocking.

The cornice shown in this project starts with a 1⅜" colonial stop installed along the ceiling and a band of 3¼" colonial baseboard run along the wall. A simple crown molding is then fastened to the two moldings to complete the cornice.

An air nailer is especially useful for installing multiple moldings; it will be worth it to rent one for a day if your project is sizable. Of course, you can also hand-drive the nails. For additional help with measuring, cutting, and nailing your moldings, see pages 107 to 112.

Everything You Need

Tools: Power miter saw, chalk line, pneumatic finish nailer, nail set.

Materials: Wood glue, molding, 2" and 1¼" finish nails, construction adhesive.

How to Create a Built-up Cornice

1 Cut a 4"- to 6"-long piece from each type of molding. Glue or nail the pieces together in the desired arrangement to create a marking template. Position the template flush with the wall and ceiling and mark along the outside edges of the ceiling and wall moldings. Mark at both ends of each wall.

2 Locate and mark all of the wall studs and ceiling joists (see page 110), marking in areas that will be hidden by the crown molding. Snap chalk lines between the template marks you made in step 1 (you can also mark with a pencil and level). If the ceiling has a deep texture, scrape off the texture just behind the chalk lines, using a drywall taping knife.

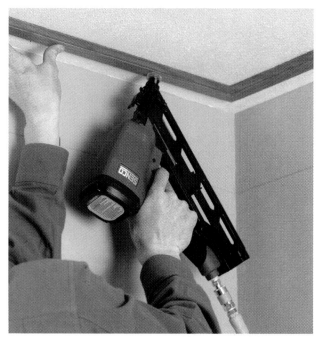

3 Install the ceiling trim, aligning its outside edge with the chalk line. Nail into the joists with 2" (6d) finish nails, and miter the joints at the inside and outside corners. Wherever possible, place the nails where they'll be hidden by the crown molding.

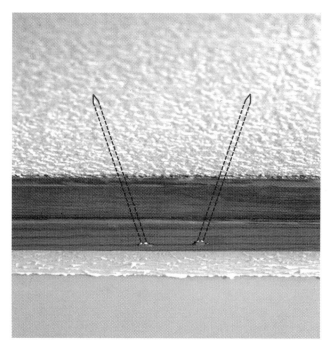

Variation: Where walls run parallel to the ceiling joists, and there are no joists to nail into, apply a bead of construction adhesive to the trim and nail it in place with pairs of nails driven at opposing angles. If you're handnailing, drill oversized pilot holes and secure the trim with coarse-thread drywall screws. Let the adhesive dry before starting the next step.

4 Install the vertical band trim along the walls, nailing into each stud with two 2" nails. Miter the band at outside corners, and miter or cope the joints at inside corners.

5 Add the crown molding, fastening it to the ceiling trim and wall band with 1¼" (3d) nails. Miter the molding at outside corners, and miter or cope the inside corners. Use a nail set to set all nails that aren't countersunk.

CORNICE VARIATIONS

Use picture rail (page 106) to enhance a cornice molding. Standard height for picture rail is about 10" to 12" below the ceiling, but you can place it at any level. For a simple variation of the project shown, use square-edged stock for the band (since the bottom edge will mostly be hidden), and add picture rail just below the band. Be sure to leave enough room for placing picture hooks.

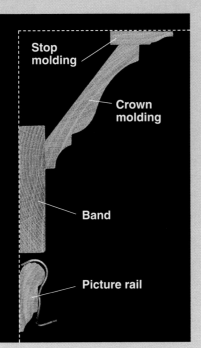

Stop molding

Crown molding

Band

Picture rail

Install blocking to provide a nailing surface and added bulk to a built-up cornice. In this simple arrangement, a 2 × 2 block, or nailing strip, is screwed to the wall studs. A facing made from 1 × 2 finish lumber is nailed to the blocking and is trimmed along the ceiling with quarter-round. The crown molding is nailed to the wall studs along the bottom and to the nailer along the top.

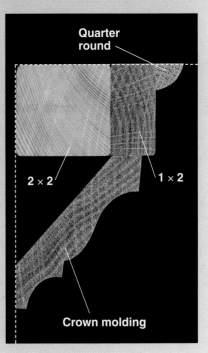

Quarter round

2 × 2

1 × 2

Crown molding

Installing Polymer Crown Molding

Polymer moldings come in a variety of ornate, single-piece styles that offer easy installation and maintenance. The polystyrene or polyurethane material is as easy to cut as softwood, but unlike wood, the material won't shrink, and it can be repaired with vinyl spackling compound.

You can buy polymer moldings preprimed for painting, or you can stain it with a non-penetrating heavy-body stain or gel. Most polymers come in 12-ft. lengths, and some have corner blocks that eliminate corner cuts. There are even flexible moldings for curved walls (see page 140).

Everything You Need

Tools: Drill with countersink-piloting bit, power miter saw or hand miter box and fine-tooth saw, caulk gun, putty knife.

Materials: Crown molding, finish nails, 150-grit sandpaper, rag, mineral spirits, polymer adhesive, 2" drywall screws, vinyl spackling compound, paintable latex caulk.

How to Install Polymer Crown Molding

1 Plan the layout of the molding pieces by measuring the walls of the room and making light pencil marks at the joint locations. For each piece that starts or ends at a corner, add 12" to 24" to compensate for waste. If possible, avoid pieces shorter than 36", because short pieces are more difficult to fit.

2 Hold a section of molding against the wall and ceiling in the finished position. Make light pencil marks on the wall every 12" along the bottom edge of the molding. Remove the molding, and tack a finish nail at each mark. The nails will hold the molding in place while the adhesive dries. If the wall surface is plaster, drill pilot holes for the nails.

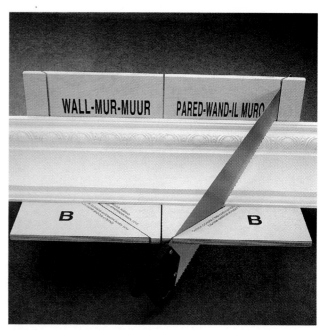

3 To make the miter cuts for the first corner, position the molding faceup in a miter box. Set the ceiling side of the molding against the horizontal table of the miter box, and set the wall side against the vertical back fence (see page 112). Make the cut at 45°.

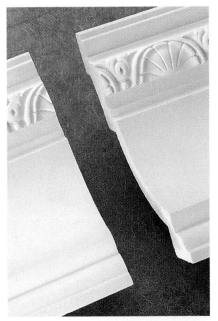

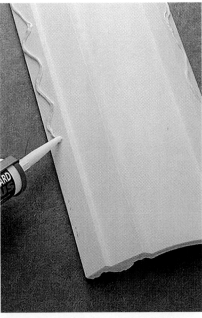

4 Check the uncut ends of each molding piece before installing it. Make sure mating pieces will butt together squarely in a tight joint. Cut all square ends at 90°, using a miter saw or hand miter box.

5 Lightly sand the backs of the molding that will contact the wall and ceiling, using 150-grit sandpaper. Slightly dampen a rag with mineral spirits, and wipe away the dust. Run a small bead of polymer adhesive (recommended or supplied by the manufacturer) along both sanded edges.

6 Set the molding in place with the mitered end tight to the corner and the bottom edge resting on the nails. Press along the molding edges to create a good bond. At each end of the piece, drive 2" drywall screws through countersunk pilot holes through the flats and into the ceiling and wall.

7 Cut, sand, and glue the next piece of molding. Apply a bead of adhesive to the end where the installed molding will meet the new piece. Install the new piece, and secure the ends with screws, making sure the ends are joined properly. Install the remaining molding pieces, and let the adhesive dry.

8 Carefully remove the finish nails and fill the nail holes with vinyl spackling compound. Fill the screw holes in the molding and any gaps in the joints with paintable latex caulk or filler, and wipe away excess caulk with a damp cloth or a wet finger. Smooth the caulk over the holes so it's flush with the surface.

Installing Door & Window Casing

Casing is the decorative molding that covers the gaps around the edges of door and window jambs. You can find casing in almost any style and in many different materials, including pine, hardwoods, and synthetic materials.

In most situations, it's easiest to paint the walls before you install the casing. You can also save time by pre-painting or staining the casing before cutting and installing it. For precise miter cuts that make tight joints, use a power miter saw, if you have one; otherwise, make cuts with a hand miter box (see page 107).

Everything You Need

Tools: Straightedge, power miter saw or miter box and backsaw, drill, nail set.

Materials: Casing, 6d and 4d finish nails, wood putty.

How to Install Door & Window Casing

1 On the front edge of each jamb, mark a reveal line to represent the inside edge of the casing. The typical reveal is around ⅛". You can set the reveal anywhere you like, but make sure it's equal on all jambs. Mark light pencil lines just at the corners, or use a straightedge to draw longer lines.

2 Place a length of casing along one side jamb, flush with the reveal line. At the top and bottom of the molding, mark the points where the horizontal and vertical reveal lines meet (with doors, mark the top ends only).

3 Make 45° miter cuts at the ends of the moldings. Measure and cut the second vertical molding piece, using the same methods.

4 Tack each vertical piece in place with two 4d finish nails driven through the casing and into the jamb. Drill pilot holes for the nails to prevent splitting. Do not drive the nails flush at this step.

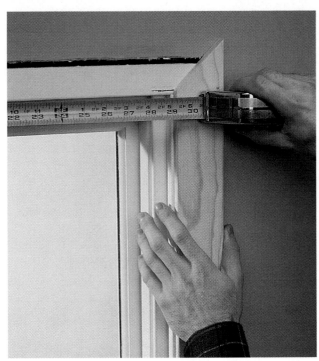

5 Measure between the vertical pieces, and cut the top and bottom pieces to length. If the joints don't fit well, move the molding pieces slightly, or make new cuts. When all of the pieces fit well, attach the casing to the jambs with 4d finish nails, spaced every 12" to 16". Then, drive 6d finish nails through the casing near the outer edge and into the wall framing.

6 Lock-nail the corner joints by drilling a pilot hole and driving a 4d finish nail through each corner, as shown. Drive all nail heads below the wood surface, using a nail set, then fill the nail holes with wood putty.

Installing Wall Frame Moldings

Adding wall frame moldings is a traditional decorative technique used to highlight special features of a room, divide large walls into smaller sections, or simply to add interest to plain surfaces. You can paint the molding the same color as the walls or use a contrasting color. For even greater contrast, paint or wallcover the areas within the frames.

Decorative wood moldings with curved contours work best for wall frames. Chair rail, picture rail, base shoe, cove, quarter-round, and other suitable molding types are readily available at home centers and lumberyards in several wood species.

To determine the sizes and locations of the frames, cut strips of paper to the width of the molding and tape them to the wall. You may want the frames to match the dimensions of architectural details in the room, such as windows or a fireplace.

Install the molding with small finish nails driven at each wall stud location and at the ends of the pieces (see page 110 for help with finding studs). Use nails long enough to penetrate the studs by ¾". If there aren't studs where you need them, secure the molding with dabs of construction adhesive.

Everything You Need

Tools: Level, framing square, miter box and backsaw, drill and bits, nail set.

Materials: Paper strips, tape, wood finishing materials, construction adhesive, paintable latex caulk or wood putty.

How to Install Wall Frame Moldings

1 Cut paper strips to the width of the molding, and tape them to the wall. Use a framing square and level to make sure the frame is level and the strips are square to one another. Mark the outer corners of the frame with light pencil lines.

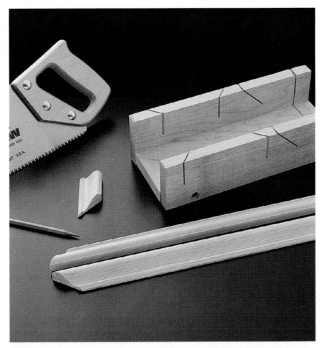

2 Cut the molding pieces to length, using a miter box and a backsaw (or power miter saw) to cut the ends at 45°. The top and bottom pieces should be the same length, as should the side pieces. Test fit the pieces, and make any necessary adjustments.

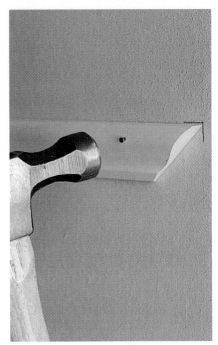

3 Paint or stain the moldings as desired. Position the top molding piece on the placement marks and tack it in place with two finish nails. If necessary, drill pilot holes for the nails to prevent splitting.

4 Tack the side moldings in place, using the framing square to make sure they are square to the top piece. Tack up the bottom piece. Adjust the frame, if necessary, so that all of the joints fit tightly, then completely fasten the pieces.

5 Drive the nails slightly below the surface, using a nail set (page 107). Fill the nail holes (and corner joints, if necessary) with paintable latex caulk, if the molding is painted, or wood putty, if it is stained. Touch up the patched areas with paint or stain.

Adding a Wainscot

A wainscot, by definition, is a wall treatment covering the lower portion of a wall. Virtually any material can be used as wainscoting, but the most common by far is wood. In most applications, the wainscot is covered along the bottom by a baseboard and along the top by a cap molding, rail, or shallow shelf.

Wainscots are useful not only for decoration but also as protective surfaces. Standard wainscot heights are between 32" and 36", a range at which the top cap can serve as a chair rail to protect the wall from furniture collisions. In hallways, mudrooms, and other functional areas, wainscots may run 48" and higher.

Wood wainscoting is available in a variety of species and styles. For price and ease of installation, the best types for do-it-yourselfers are 4 × 8-ft. sheets and tongue-&-groove boards, commonly called *beadboard*. Standard materials include paint-grade pine (and other softwoods); hardwood veneers, such as oak and birch; molded polymers; and fiberboard.

There are two basic methods for installing wainscoting. Sheets and thinner boards (up to ⅜", in most cases) can be attached to drywall with construction adhesive and nails, or with nails alone. Thicker boards usually must be nailed, preferably blind-nailed—the technique of driving angled nails along the base of the tongue so the groove of the next board hides the nail heads. Thinner boards may have to be face-nailed to avoid splitting the wood.

Wainscoting that is fastened only with nails must have blocking or backing to serve as a nailing surface. If the framing is exposed, you can install plywood backing over the wall studs in the area of the wainscot, then cover the rest of the wall with drywall of the same thickness (make sure the local building code permits installing wood directly over wall framing). You can also install 2 × 4 blocks between the studs, at 12" to 16" intervals, before hanging the drywall.

The project on pages 123 to 124 shows you how to install a tall wainscot of sheet paneling with a traditional molding treatment. A rail made from 1 × 6 clear pine runs along the top edge of paneling and is topped by a 1 × 3 pine cap with custom edges you mill with a router. Because of its height (60") and tall baseboard, this wainscot is especially suited to mudroom or hallway walls that receive some abuse, but it can work well in

bathrooms and other areas. You can install hooks for coats (or towels) along the rail or add a shelf for additional storage.

Everything You Need

Tools: Chalk line, level, circular saw, caulk gun, drill, router with roundover bit, power miter saw, nail set.

Materials: Sheet paneling; construction adhesive; 10d, 6d, and 2d finish nails; 1 × 6 and 1 × 3 clear pine lumber; wood glue; cove molding; baseboard.

How to Install a Wainscot with Sheet Paneling

1 Measure up from the floor and snap a chalk line to represent the top of the paneling. This line will be ¾" lower than the overall height of the wainscot. Use a pencil to mark the stud locations about 1" above the chalk line (see page 110). Measure the length of the wall to plan the layout of the sheets. The last piece should be at least 3" wide, so you may have to trim the first sheet to make the last piece wider.

2 Check the wall corner with a level to make sure it's plumb. If it's not plumb, scribe the first sheet to follow the angle or contours of the wall (see Tip, page 125). Cut the first sheet to length so its bottom edge will be ½" above the floor, using a circular saw. Unless you've scribed the sheet, cut from the back side to prevent splintering on the face. Using a caulk gun, apply construction adhesive to the back side.

3 Apply the sheet to the wall so its top edge is flush with the chalk line and its side edge is set into the corner. Press the sheet firmly to bond it to the wall. Drive 6d finish nails at the stud locations, spacing them every 16", or so. Use only as many nails as needed to hold the sheet flat and to keep it in place.

4 Install the remaining sheets in the wall section. If you are paneling an adjacent wall, check the paneled wall for plumb, and trim the first sheet, if necessary. Install the sheet butted against the end sheet on the paneled wall.

(continued next page)

5 Prepare the 1 × 6 rail material by sanding smooth the front face and bottom edge. If desired, round over the bottom, outside corner slightly with sand paper. Install the rail with its top edge flush with the chalk line, fastening it to each stud with two 10d finish nails driven through pilot holes. Butt together rail pieces at inside corners, and miter them at outside corners, following the same techniques used for cutting and fitting baseboard (see pages 108 and 111).

6 Mill the 1 × 3 top cap material, using a router and roundover bit. Work on test pieces to find the desired amount of roundover, then rout your workpieces on both front corners. Sand the cap smooth. OPTION: Create a waterfall edge by rounding over only the top edge of the cap (top inset), or chamfer the front edges with a chamfer bit (bottom inset).

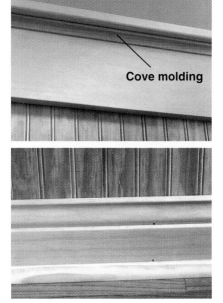

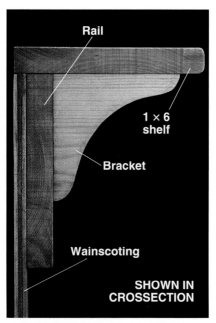

7 Install the cap with wood glue and finish nails. Glue along the top edge of the rail and drive a 10d finish nail, angled at 45° through the cap and into each stud (drill pilot holes for the nails). Miter the rail at corners.

8 Add cove molding to the joint between the cap and rail, fastening it to the rail with 2d finish nails. Install the baseboard along the bottom of the wainscot (see page 111). Set all nails with a nail set (see page 107).

Variation: Top your wainscot with a shelf rather than a cap. Use 1 × 6 or wider boards, and mill them as shown in step 6. To support the shelf, add wooden brackets fastened to the wall studs.

124

Tips for Installing Tongue-&-Groove Wainscoting

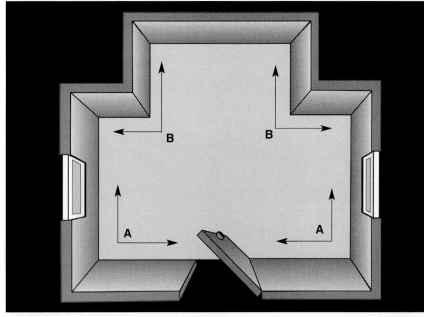

Begin your installation at the corners, either inside (A) or outside (B). Use the reveal dimension (see pages 126 to 127) to calculate the number of boards required for each wall: divide the length of the wall by the reveal, keeping in mind that a side edge may have to be trimmed from one or more of the corner boards. If the total number of boards includes a fraction of less than half a board, plan to trim the first board to avoid ending with a board cut to less than half its original width.

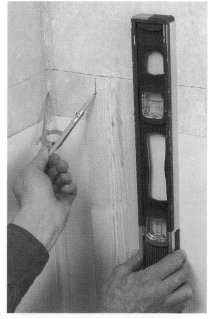

Check corners for plumb. If a corner isn't plumb, scribe and trim the first board to fit. At inside corners, use a level to hold the board plumb, then use a compass to transfer the contours of the wall to the board. At outside corners, overhang the wall edge and scribe along the board's back side.

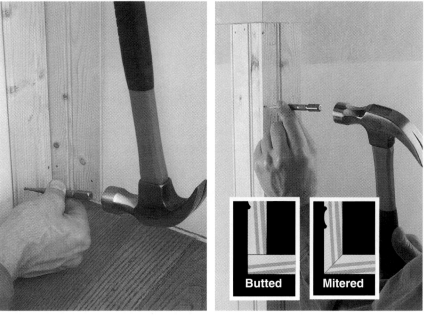

Butted Mitered

Start inside corners (left) by trimming off the tongue edge of the first board, or simply place the groove edge in the corner. Install the first board, leaving a ⅛" expansion gap in the corner. Butt the board on the adjacent wall against the face of the first board. At outside corners (right), join boards with butt joints or miter joints (insets). If necessary, drill pilot holes for the nails to prevent splitting. Drive the bottom and top nails where they'll be hidden by the molding. Set all nails with a nail set.

Install subsequent boards along the wall, following the panel manufacturer's directions regarding expansion gaps at the joints. Use a level to check every third board for plumb. If it's out of plumb, adjust the fourth board to compensate.

Paneling a Ceiling

©Karen Melvin

Tongue-&-groove paneling offers a warm, attractive finish that's especially suited to vaulted ceilings. Pine is the most common material for tongue-&-groove paneling, but you can choose from many different wood species and panel styles. Panels typically are ⅜" to ¾" thick and are often attached directly to ceiling joists or rafters. Some building codes require the installation of drywall as a fire stop behind ceiling paneling that's thinner than ¼".

When purchasing your paneling, get enough material to cover about 15% more square footage than the actual ceiling size, to allow for waste. Since the tongue portions of the panels slip into the grooves of adjacent pieces, square footage for paneling is based on the *reveal*—the exposed face of the panel after it is installed.

Tongue-&-groove boards can be attached with flooring nails or finish nails. Flooring nails hold better because they have spiraled shanks, but they tend to have larger heads than finish nails. Whenever possible, drive the nails through the base of the tongue and into the framing. This is called *blind-nailing,* because the groove of the succeeding board covers the nail heads. Add facenails only at joints and in locations where more support is needed, such as along the first and last boards. To ensure clean cuts, use a compound miter saw. These saws are especially useful for ceilings with non-90° angles.

Layout is crucial to the success of a paneling project. Before you start, determine how many boards you'll need, using the reveal measurement. If the final board will be less than 2" wide, trim the first, or *starter*, board by cutting the long edge that abuts the wall. If the ceiling peak is not parallel to the side (starting) wall, rip the starter piece at an angle to match the wall. The leading edge of the starter piece, and every piece thereafter, must be parallel to the peak.

Everything You Need

Tools: Chalk line, compound miter saw, circular saw, drill, nail set.

Materials: Tongue-&-groove paneling, 1¾" spiral flooring nails, trim molding.

How to Panel a Ceiling

1 To plan your layout, first measure the reveal of the boards. Fit two pieces together and measure from the bottom edge of the upper board to the bottom edge of the lower board. Calculate the number of boards needed to cover one side of the ceiling by dividing the reveal dimension into the overall distance between the top of the wall and the peak.

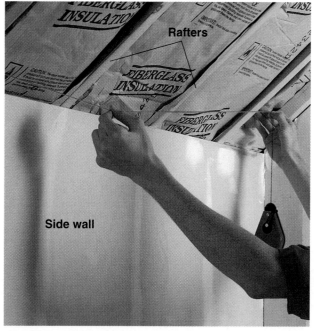

2 Use the calculation from step 1 to make a control line for the first row of panels—the starter boards. At both ends of the ceiling, measure down from the peak an equal distance, and make a mark to represent the top (tongue) edges of the starter boards. Snap a chalk line through the marks.

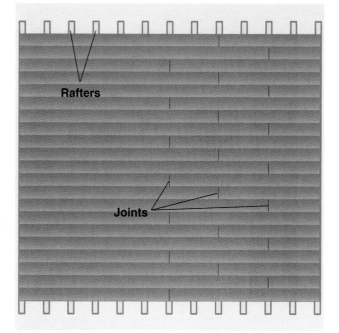

3 If the boards aren't long enough to span the entire ceiling, plan the locations of the joints. Staggering the joints in a three-step pattern will make them less conspicuous. Note that each joint must fall over the middle of a rafter. For best appearance, select boards of similar coloring and grain for each row.

4 Rip the first starter board to width by bevel-cutting the bottom (grooved) edge. If the starter row will have joints, cut the board to length using a 30° bevel cut on the joint end only. Two beveled ends joined together form a *scarf* joint (inset), which is less noticeable than a butt joint. If the board spans the ceiling, square-cut both ends.

(continued next page)

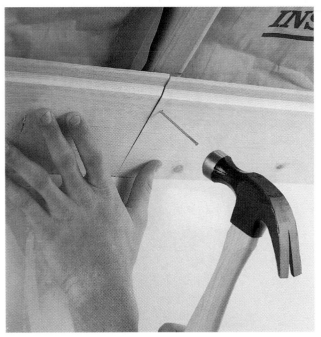

5 Position the first starter board so the tongue is on the control line. Leave a ⅛" gap between the square board end and the end wall. Fasten the board by nailing through its face about 1" from the grooved edge and into the rafters. Then, blind-nail through the base of the tongue into each rafter, angling the nail backward at 45°. Drive the nail heads beneath the wood surface, using a nail set.

6 Cut and install any remaining boards in the starter row one at a time, making sure the scarf joints fit together tightly. At each scarf joint, drive two nails through the face of the top board, angling the nail to capture the end of the board behind it. If necessary, predrill the nail holes to prevent splitting.

7 Cut the first board for the next row, then fit its grooved edge over the tongue of the board in the starter row. Use a hammer and a scrap piece of paneling to drive downward on the tongue edge, seating the grooved edge over the tongue of the starter board. Fasten the second row with blind-nails only.

8 As you install successive rows, measure down from the peak to make sure the rows remain parallel to the peak. Correct any misalignment by adjusting the tongue-&-groove joint slightly with each row. You can also snap additional control lines to help align the rows.

9 Rip the boards for the last row to width, beveling the top edges so they fit flush against the ridge board. Facenail the boards in place. Install paneling on the other side of the ceiling, then cut and install the final row of panels to form a closed joint under the ridge board (inset).

10 Install trim molding along walls, at joints around obstacles, and along inside and outside corners, if desired. (Select-grade 1 × 2 works well as trim along walls.) Where necessary, bevel the back edges of the trim or miter-cut the ends to accommodate the slope of the ceiling.

Tips for Paneling an Attic Ceiling

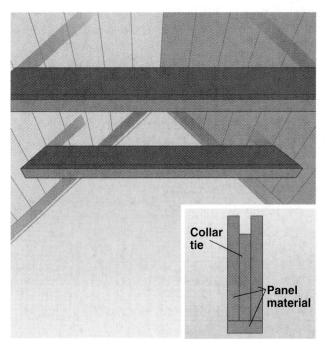

Use mitered trim to cover joints where panels meet at outside corners. Dormers and other roof elements create opposing ceiling angles that can be difficult to panel around. It may be easier to butt the panels together and hide the butt joints with custom-cut trim. The trim also makes a nice transition between angles.

Wrap collar ties or exposed beams with custom-cut panels. Install the paneling on the ceiling first. Then, rip-cut panels to the desired width. You may want to include a tongue-&-groove joint as part of the trim detail. Angle-cut the ends of the trim so it fits tight to the ceiling panels.

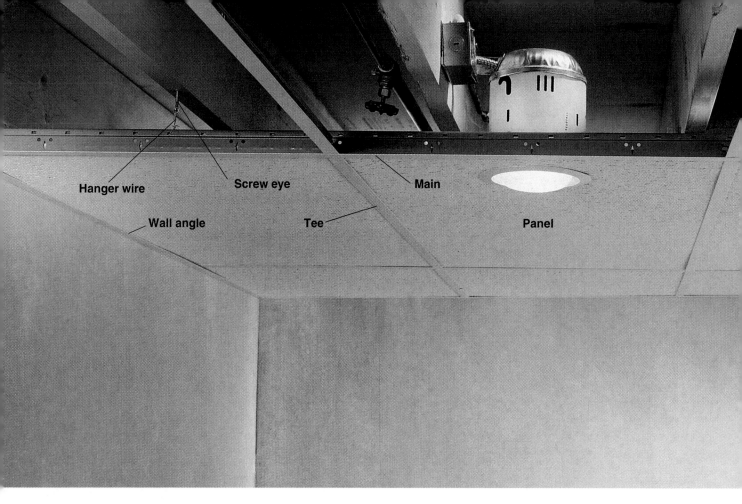

Hanger wire   Screw eye   Main

Wall angle   Tee   Panel

Installing a Suspended Ceiling

Suspended ceilings are popular ceiling finishes for basements and utility areas, particularly because they hang below pipes and ducts while providing easy access to them. And, unlike drywall, suspended ceilings aren't affected by uneven joists. However, because they should hang about 4" below the lowest obstacle (to provide room for installing or removing the panels), suspended ceilings take up more headroom, so make sure your finished ceiling height will comply with the local building code.

A suspended ceiling is a grid framework made of lightweight metal brackets hung on wires attached to ceiling or floor joists. The frame consists of T-shaped main beams (mains), cross-tees (tees), and L-shaped wall angles. The grid supports ceiling panels, which rest on the flanges of the framing pieces. Panels are available in 2 × 2-ft. or 2 × 4-ft. sizes, in a variety of styles. Special options include insulated panels, acoustical panels that absorb sound, and light-diffuser screens for use with fluorescent lights. Generally, metal-frame ceiling systems are more durable than ones made of plastic.

To begin your ceiling project, devise the panel layout based on the size of the room, placing equally sized trimmed panels on opposite sides to create a balanced look. Your ceiling must also be level. For small rooms, a 4-ft. or 6-ft. level will work, but a water level is more effective for larger jobs. You can make a water level with two water-level ends (available at hardware stores and home centers) attached to a standard garden hose.

Although suspended ceilings work well for hiding mechanicals in a basement, it looks best if you build soffits around low obstructions, such as support beams and large ducts (see pages 23 to 25). Finish the soffits with drywall, and install the ceiling wall angle to the soffit.

Everything You Need

Tools: Water level, chalk line, drill, aviation snips, dryline, lock-type clamps, screw-eye driver, pliers, straightedge, utility knife.

Materials: Suspended ceiling kit (frame), screw eyes, hanger wires, ceiling panels, 1½" drywall screws or masonry nails.

Tips for Installing a Suspended Ceiling

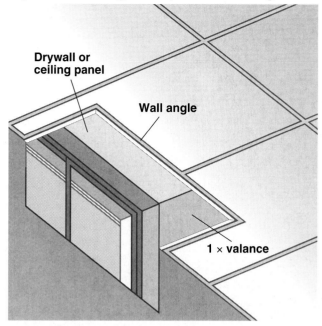

Drywall or ceiling panel

Wall angle

1 × valance

Build a valance around basement awning windows so they can be opened fully. Attach 1 × lumber of an appropriate width to joists or blocking. Install drywall (or a suspended-ceiling panel trimmed to fit) to the joists inside the valance.

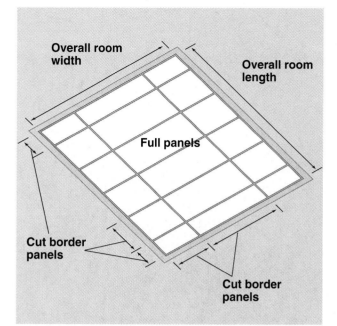

Overall room width

Overall room length

Full panels

Cut border panels

Cut border panels

Draw your ceiling layout on paper, based on the exact dimensions of the room. Plan so that trimmed border panels on opposite sides of the room are of equal width and length (avoid panels smaller than ½-size). If you include lighting fixtures in your plan, make sure they follow the grid layout.

How to Install a Suspended Ceiling

1 Make a mark on one wall that represents the ceiling height plus the height of the wall angle. Use a water level to transfer that height to both ends of each wall. Snap a chalk line to connect the marks. This line represents the top of the ceiling's wall angle.

2 Attach wall angle pieces to the studs on all walls, positioning the top of the wall angle flush with the chalk line. Use 1½" drywall screws (or short masonry nails driven into mortar joints on concrete block walls). Cut angle pieces using aviation snips.

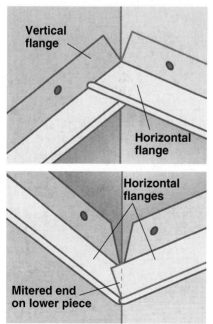

Vertical flange

Horizontal flange

Horizontal flanges

Mitered end on lower piece

Tip: Trim wall angle pieces to fit around corners. At inside corners (top), back-cut the vertical flanges slightly, then overlap the horizontal flanges. At outside corners (bottom), miter-cut one horizontal flange, and overlap the flanges.

(continued next page)

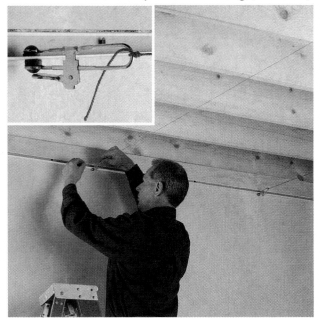

3 Mark the location of each main on the wall angles at the ends of the room. The mains must be parallel to each other and perpendicular to the ceiling joists. Set up a guide string for each main, using a thin dryline and lock-type clamps (inset). Clamp the strings to the opposing wall angles, stretching them very taut so there's no sagging.

4 Install screw eyes for hanging the mains, using a drill and screw-eye driver. Drill pilot holes and drive the eyes into the joists every 4 ft., locating them directly above the guide strings. Attach hanger wire to the screw eyes by threading one end through the eye and twisting the wire on itself at least three times. Trim excess wire, leaving a few inches of wire hanging below the level of the guide string.

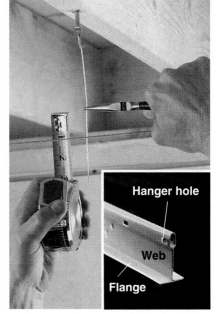

Hanger hole

Web

Flange

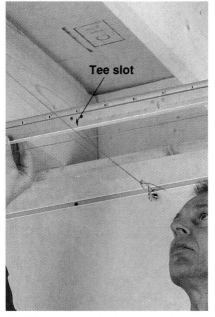

Tee slot

5 Measure the distance from the bottom of a main's flange to the hanger hole in the web (inset). Use this measurement to prebend each hanger wire. Measure up from the guide string and make a 90° bend in the wire, using pliers.

6 Following your ceiling plan, mark the placement of the first tee on opposite wall angles at one end of the room. Set up a guide string for the tee, using a dryline and clamps, as before. This string must be perpendicular to the guide strings for the mains.

7 Trim one end of each main so that a tee slot in the main's web is aligned with the tee guide string, and the end of the main bears fully on a wall angle. Set the main in place to check the alignment of the tee slot with the string.

8 Cut the other end of each main to fit, so that it rests on the opposing wall angle. If a single main cannot span the room, splice two mains together, end-to-end (the ends should be fashioned with male-female connectors). Make sure the tee slots remain aligned when splicing.

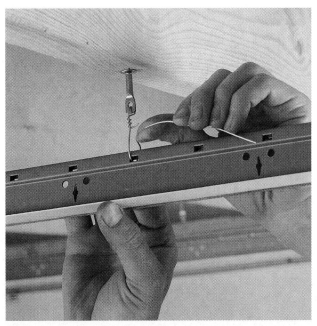

9 Install the mains by setting the ends on the wall angle and threading the hanger wires through the hanger holes in the webs. The wires should be as close to vertical as possible. Wrap each wire around itself three times, making sure the main's flange is level with the main guide string. Also install a hanger near each main splice.

10 Attach tees to the mains, slipping their tabbed ends into the tee slots on the mains. Align the first row of tees with the tee guide string; install the remaining rows at 4-ft. intervals. If you're using 2 × 2-ft. panels, install 2-ft. cross-tees between the midpoints of the 4-ft. tees. Cut and install the border tees, setting the tee ends on the wall angles. Remove all guide strings and clamps.

11 Place full ceiling panels into the grid first, then install the border panels. Lift the panels in at an angle, and position them so they rest on the frame's flanges. Reach through adjacent openings to adjust the panels, if necessary. To trim the border panels to size, cut them faceup, using a straightedge and utility knife (inset).

Installing Ceiling Tile

Photo courtesy of Armstrong Ceilings

Easy-to-install ceiling tile can lend character to a plain ceiling or help turn an unfinished basement or attic into beautiful living space. Made of pressed mineral and fiberboard, ceiling tiles are available in a variety of styles. They also provide moderate noise reduction.

Ceiling tiles typically can be attached directly to a drywall or plaster ceiling with adhesive. If your ceiling is damaged or uneven, or if you have an unfinished joist ceiling, install 1 × 2 furring strips as a base for the tiles, as shown in this project. Some systems include metal tracks for clip-on installation.

Unless your ceiling measures in even feet, you won't be able to install the 12" tiles without some cutting. To prevent an unattractive installation with small, irregular tiles along two sides, include a course of border tiles along the perimeter of the installation. Plan so that tiles at opposite ends of the room are cut to the same width and are at least ½ the width of a full tile.

Most ceiling tile comes prefinished, but it can be painted to match any decor. For best results, apply two coats of paint using a roller with a ¼" nap, and wait 24 hours between coats.

Everything You Need

Tools: 4-ft. level, stepladder, chalk line, utility knife, straightedge, hammer or drill, handsaw, stapler.

Materials: 1 × 2 furring strips, 8d nails or 2" screws, string, ceiling tiles, staples, trim molding.

Create an area rug effect by covering only a portion of the ceiling with tiles. This technique helps to define living areas in open floor plans by breaking up bland expanses of white ceiling.

Photo courtesy of Armstrong Ceilings

Add a faux patina by randomly dabbing the tiles with metallic green or blue paint, using a natural sea sponge.

How to Install Ceiling Tile

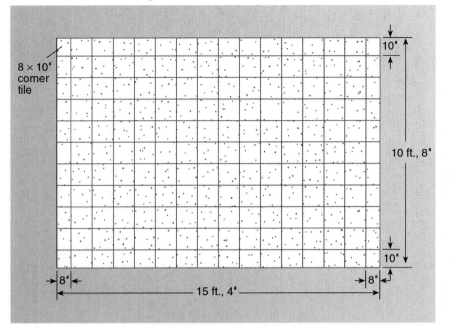

8 × 10" corner tile

10"

10 ft., 8"

10"

8"

15 ft., 4"

8"

1 Measure the ceiling and devise a layout. If the length (or width) doesn't measure in even feet, use this formula to determine the width of the border tiles: add 12 to the number of inches remaining and divide by 2. The result is the width of the border tile. (For example, if the room length is 15 ft., 4", add 12 to the 4, then divide 16 by 2, which results in an 8" border tile.)

2 Install the first furring strip flush with the wall and perpendicular to the joists, fastening with two 8d nails or 2" screws at each joist. Measure out from the wall a distance equal to the border tile width minus ¾", and snap a chalk line. Install the second furring strip with its wall-side edge on the chalk line.

3 Install the remaining strips 12" on-center from the second strip. Measure from the second strip and mark the joist nearest the wall every 12". Repeat along the joist on the opposite side of the room, then snap chalk lines between the marks. Install the furring strips along the lines. Install the last furring strip flush against the opposite side wall. Stagger the butted end joints of strips between rows so they aren't all on the same joist.

4 Check the strips with a 4-ft. level. Insert wood shims between the strips and joists as necessary to bring the strips into a level plane.

(continued next page)

5 Set up taut, perpendicular string lines along two adjacent walls to help guide the tile installation. Inset the strings from the wall by a distance that equals that wall's border tile width plus ½". Use a framing square to make sure the strings are square.

6 Cut the corner border tile to size with a utility knife and straightedge. Cutting the border tiles ¼" short will ease fitting them. The resulting gap between the tile and wall will be covered by trim. Cut only on the edges without the stapling flange.

7 Position the corner tile with the flange edges aligned with the two string lines and fasten it to the furring strips with four ½" staples. Cut and install two border tiles along each wall, making sure the tiles fit snugly together.

8 Fill in between the border tiles with full-size tiles. Continue working diagonally in this manner, toward the opposite corner. For the border tiles along the far wall, trim off the flange edges and staple through the faces of the tiles, close to the wall.

9 Install the final row of tiles, saving the far corner tile and its neighbor for last. Cut the last tile to size, then remove the tongue and nailing flange along the side edges. Finish the job by installing trim along the edges (see pages 106 to 112).

Photo courtesy of Brian Greer's Tin-Ceilings

Installing a Metal Tile Ceiling

Today's metal ceilings offer the distinctive elegance of 19th-century tin tile in a durable, washable ceiling finish. Available at home centers and specialty distributors, metal ceiling systems include field panels (in 2 × 2-, 2 × 4-, and 2 × 8-ft. sizes), border panels that can be cut to fit your layout, and cornice molding for finishing the edges. The panels come in a variety of materials and finishes ready for installation, or they can be painted.

To simplify installation, the panels have round catches, called nailing buttons, that fit into one another to align the panels where they overlap. The buttons are also the nailing points for attaching the panels. Use 1" decorative conehead nails where nail heads will be exposed, and ½" wire nails where heads are hidden.

Install your metal ceiling over a smooth layer of ⅜" or ½" plywood, which can be fastened directly to the ceiling joists with drywall screws, or installed over an existing finish. The plywood pro-

vides a flat nailing surface for the panels. As an alternative, some manufacturers offer a track system for clip-on installation.

Begin your installation by carefully measuring the ceiling and snapping chalk lines to establish the panel layout. For most tile patterns, it looks best to cover the center of the space with full tiles only, then fill in along the perimeter with border panels, which are not patterned. Make sure your layout is square.

Everything You Need

Tools: Chalk line, level, tin snips, drill with ⅛" metal bit, compass, metal file.

Materials: ⅜" or ½" plywood, 2" drywall screws, field panels, border panels with molding edge, cornice molding, masking tape, ½" wire nails, 1" conehead nails, wood block.

How to Install a Metal Tile Ceiling

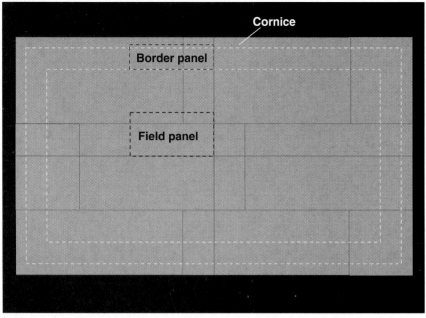

1 Measure to find the center of the ceiling, then snap perpendicular chalk lines intersecting the center. On the walls, mark a level reference line representing the bottom edges of the cornice molding. Where possible, plan to install the panels so they overlap toward the room's entrance, to help conceal the seams.

2 Align the first field panel with the chalk lines at the ceiling's center, and attach it with ½" wire nails along the edges where another panel will overlap it. Drive the nails beside the nailing buttons—saving the buttons for nailing the overlapping panel.

3 Continue to install field panels, working along the length of the area first, then overlapping the next row. Make sure the nailing buttons are aligned. Underlap panels by sliding the new panel into position beneath the installed panel, then fasten through both panels at the nailing buttons, using 1" conehead nails. Where field panels meet at corners, drill ⅛" pilot holes for the conehead nails.

4 Cut the border panels to width so they will underlap the cornice by at least 1". Use sharp tin snips, and cut from the edge without edge molding. Install the panels so the nailing buttons on the molding align with those on the field panels. Fasten through the buttons with conehead nails, and along the cut edge with wire nails. At corners, miter-cut the panels, and drive conehead nails every 6" along the seam.

138

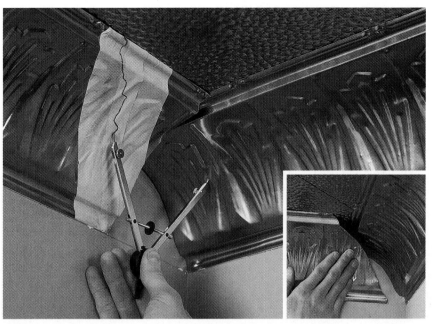

5 Install each cornice piece with its bottom edge on the level line. Drive 1" conehead nails through the nailing buttons and into the wall studs. Don't nail the ends until the succeeding piece is in place. Fasten the top edges to the ceiling.

6 At inside corners, install one cornice piece tightly into the corner, then scribe the mating piece to fit, using masking tape and a compass. Cut along the scribed line with tin snips, and make minor adjustments with a metal file. You may have to cut the mating piece several times, so start with plenty of length. If you have several corners, use this technique to cut templates for the corner pieces.

7 At outside corners, cut the ends of two scrap pieces at a 33° angle. Fit the pieces together at the corner, then trim and mark each piece in turn, making minor adjustments until they fit well. Use the scrap pieces as templates for marking the workpieces. Fasten near the corner only when both mating pieces are in place.

8 Using a hammer and a piece of wood, carefully tap any loose joints to tighten them. If the cornice will be left unpainted, file the joints for a perfect fit. If you're painting the ceiling, seal the seams with paintable silicone caulk, then apply two coats of paint using a roller with a ¼" nap. Allow the first coat to dry for 24 hours before applying the second coat.

Metric Conversions

To Convert:	To:	Multiply by:
Inches	Millimeters	25.4
Inches	Centimeters	2.54
Feet	Meters	0.305
Yards	Meters	0.914
Square inches	Square centimeters	6.45
Square feet	Square meters	0.093
Square yards	Square meters	0.836
Ounces	Milliliters	30.0
Pints (U.S.)	Liters	0.473 (Imp. 0.568)
Quarts (U.S.)	Liters	0.946 (Imp. 1.136)
Gallons (U.S.)	Liters	3.785 (Imp. 4.546)
Ounces	Grams	28.4
Pounds	Kilograms	0.454

To Convert:	To:	Multiply by:
Millimeters	Inches	0.039
Centimeters	Inches	0.394
Meters	Feet	3.28
Meters	Yards	1.09
Square centimeters	Square inches	0.155
Square meters	Square feet	10.8
Square meters	Square yards	1.2
Milliliters	Ounces	.033
Liters	Pints (U.S.)	2.114 (Imp. 1.76)
Liters	Quarts (U.S.)	1.057 (Imp. 0.88)
Liters	Gallons (U.S.)	0.264 (Imp. 0.22)
Grams	Ounces	0.035
Kilograms	Pounds	2.2

Additional Resources

Flex - C Trac
(flexible track for curved walls)
405-715-1799
www.flexc.com

Georgia-Pacific
(Dens-Shield® Tile Backer,
sound-deadening gypsum board)
800-225-6119
www.gp.com

James Hardie Building Products
(Hardibacker® Fiber-cement Board)
888-JHARDIE
www.jameshardie.com

National Gypsum
800-NATIONAL
www.nationalgypsum.com

Outwater Plastics Industries Inc.
(flexible polymer molding, specialty
architectural products)
888-OUTWATER
www.outwater.com

Owens Corning
(insulation, soundproofing products)
800-GET-PINK
www.owenscorning.com

USG Corporation
(cementboard and drywall products,
soundproofing insulation)
800-USG-4YOU
www.usg.com

Photo Credits

Photo Contributors

Architectural Products by
Outwater/Orac decor
800-835-4400
www.outwater.com

Armstrong Ceilings
800-426-4261
www.armstrongceilings.com

Brian Greer's Tin-Ceilings, Walls & Unique
Metal Work
519-743-9710
www.tinceiling.com

Pittsburgh Corning Corporation
800-624-2120
www.pittsburghcorning.com

Thibaut
800-223-0704
Freulein Stripe/Stripe resource II-bath p. 4;
Fruit Bouquet Toile resource-dining p. 11

Photographers

Crandall & Crandall
Dana Point, CA
www.crandallandcrandall
©Crandall & Crandall p. 8

Karen Melvin
Architectural Stock Images, Inc.
Minneapolis, MN
©Karen Melvin: pp. 3, 8, 70-71, and for
the following designers: Jeff Ducharme,
Henderson House, MN p. 6; Sala Archi-
tects p. 7; Carol Boyles Interiors p. 10;
Tim Hartigan p. 126

Melabee M. Miller
Hillside, NJ
©Melabee Miller for the following designers: Tracey Stephens p. 6; Sandra Wilkin-
son p. 8

Robert Perron
Branford, CT
©Robert Perron: pp. 7, 9, 11

Greg Premru Photography
Boston, MA
©Greg Premru: for Amorey Architects p. 7

Holly Stickley Photography
Tigard, OR
©Holly Stickley: p. 9

Jesse Walker Associates
Glencoe, IL
©Jesse Walker: pp. 9, 11

Index

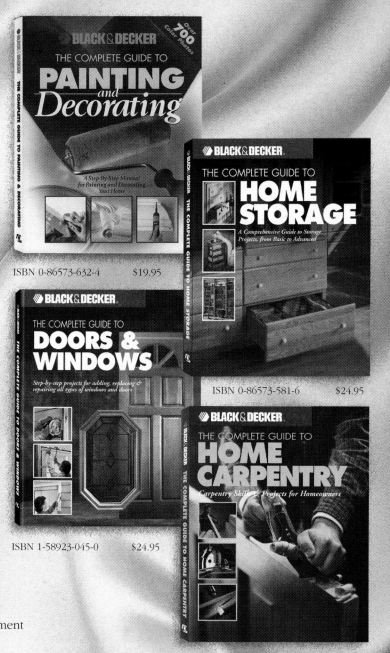